Renewing Your Mind

Among Other Books by the Author

Renewing Your Mind

Basic Christian Beliefs
You Need to Know

R. C. Sproul

Baker Books

A Division of Baker Book House Co
Grand Rapids, Michigan 49516

Third edition
Published by Baker Books
a division of Baker Book House Company
P.O. Box 6287, Grand Rapids, MI 49516-6287

First edition: *The Symbol* (1973).
Second edition: *Basic Training* (1982).

Printed in the United States of America

Library of Congress Cataloging-in-Publication Data

Sproul, R. C. (Robert Charles), 1939–
   Renewing your mind : basic Christian beliefs you need to know / R. C. Sproul.
      p.   cm.
   Rev. ed. of : Basic training, plain talk on the key truths of the faith. 1982.
   Includes bibliographical references.
   ISBN 0-8010-5815-5 (pbk.)
    1. Theology, Doctrinal—Popular works. 2. Apostles' Creed. I. Sproul, R. C. (Robert Charles), 1939– Basic training, plain talk on the key truths of the faith. II. Title.
BT77.S717   1998
238'.11—dc21   97-51406

Scripture references are from the New King James Version unless otherwise specified.

For current information about all releases from Baker Book House, visit our web site:
http://www.bakerbooks.com

For information about Ligonier Ministries and the teaching ministry of R. C. Sproul, visit Ligonier's web site:
http://www.gospelcom.net/ligonier

THE APOSTLES' CREED

I believe . . .

    in God the Father Almighty,
    Maker of heaven and earth,

and in Jesus Christ, his only Son, our Lord;
    who was
        conceived by the Holy Ghost;
        born of the virgin Mary;
        suffered under Pontius Pilate;
        was crucified, dead, and buried;
    he descended into hell;
    the third day he arose again from the dead;
    he ascended into heaven,
and sits at the right hand of God the Father Almighty;
from whence he shall come to judge the living and the dead.

I believe in . . .
    the Holy Ghost;
    the holy catholic church;
    the communion of saints;
    the forgiveness of sins;
    the resurrection of the body;
    and the life everlasting.

Amen.

Contents

Preface

Because of modern medical technology, transplanted kidneys, lungs, and even hearts provide new life for the dying. In laboratory experiments, mice have been rejuvenated by transplanted pineal glands, which reverse the aging process and extend their life expectancy by 25 percent—an experiment that hints that human life expectancy could go beyond 115 years. Such radical changes in human life stagger the imagination about what the future holds in store.

But nothing is as radical as a new mind. Yet this is not accomplished by a brain transplant, or by some technological or biological procedure. It is a matter of *theology*. To be conformed to the thinking of this world is to think with its forms or structures. To be transformed is to think beyond the forms of this world. And the power for this transformation is the renewed mind.

The renewed mind is initiated by the immediate, sovereign, supernatural work of God, the Holy Spirit, in regeneration. It is developed by the continued operation of the Spirit in the soul and by feeding upon the Word of God. It is the conformity of the believer to the person of Christ. And to have the mind of Christ is to think like Jesus. It is to love the things he loves and to eschew the things he denies.

Renewing Your Mind is a revised, updated version of the first book I ever wrote. It originally appeared under the title, *The Sym-*

bol, and later as *Basic Training in the Christian Life.* It was called *The Symbol* because it follows the outline of the classic "symbol" of the Christian faith, the Apostles' Creed.

This ancient creed summarizes the cardinal tenets of Christian belief, including those affirmations of the confessing church that capture the very essence of Christian thought and faith. It boldly declares that there is truth that is foundational to life, a truth that cannot be compromised without the peril of falling into the abyss of meaninglessness.

Any creed can be affirmed by the lips without being embraced by the heart. But once a creed is embraced by the heart, the mind is captured by it. The mind held captive by the Word of God is a transformed and transforming mind. It is a new mind that yields a new life.

To be a Christian is to be one who believes. The content of that faith is at once radical and liberating. It is the truth that sets us free!

R. C. Sproul

I believe . . .

Confess or Profess?

When a person embraces the Christian faith and says with assurance, "I believe . . . ," that person has truly embarked upon life.

The Bible describes that life as new:

- "I will put a new spirit in the people," God tells Jeremiah and Ezekiel (Jer. 31:33; Ezek. 11:19).
- To stand before God, Jesus explains, you must be "born again" (John 3:7).
- The apostle Paul describes it as "a new creation."[1]

This newness is more elemental than the latest computer software. Jesus looks us squarely in the eye in John 3 and says, "So, you think you learned what newness means when you held your first baby? That little bundle of life gave you just a glimpse of what a spiritual birth means."

Equipped with newness, a baby in Christ begins a life journey with the words "I believe. . . ." It is a pilgrimage, an adventure with both surprises and pitfalls. Moments of pain, doubt, and confusion rear up to discourage. The Christian life is nothing if not challenging. It is not the fun life, nor the easy life.

It *is* life.

This book is about living that life to the fullest, about renewing your mind so that your thinking conforms to the mind of Christ. Our spiritual creation in Christ inaugurates an intellectual and emotional creation, but does not complete it. Some old thought patterns and philosophical assumptions remain. To deal with those we need to move our metaphor of the Christian life from the nursery to boot camp. Now comes basic training in righteousness, the hard work of truth calisthenics to develop strong, disciplined faith muscles.

FORTIFIED FAITH FOR A HOSTILE WORLD

Some companies set up a gym or weight room, build a running track, or offer employees membership in a health club. Physical well-being contributes to mental and emotional health and makes for a happier, more productive employee. God pioneered on-the-job fitness training for building up the Christian. Faith must be lived in the context of a world of unbelief. So that world is where the Christian works out. It is a difficult regimen, but an easier training camp would not push the Christian beyond the limits of self-sufficiency. The duress of living in the midst of a hostile world tests and proves what is genuine. Nothing contrived will stand.

I Believe . . .

The setting for living and learning "I believe . . ." faith today is interesting, if difficult. The Church of the Iron Oak has a page on the World Wide Web promoting its belief in the precepts of witchcraft and druidry. Hare Krishna's internet page stands alongside

Jews for Jesus, the Church of Satan, and the Southern Baptists. One study counted the number of web page references to God or gods and found more than 42,000. That was second only to references to sex, of which there were more than 46,000.

A Time–CNN poll found that 82 percent of those surveyed believe in the healing power of personal prayer, while 77 percent think that God sometimes intervenes to cure serious illness. On the same page of *Time* on which that high view of prayer was reported, film producer Marty Kaplan testified to his own journey from Judaism to atheism and back again. Whether it was the editors' intent, Kaplan's statement of faith gives perspective to the survey results:

> The God I have found is common to Moses and Muhammad, to Buddha and Jesus. It is known to every mystic tradition. In mine, it is the Tetragrammaton, the Name so holy that those who know it dare not say it. It is what the Cabala calls Ayin, Nothingness, No-Thingness. It is Spirit, Being, the All. I used to think of psychic phenomena as New Age flimflam. I used to think of reincarnation as a myth. I used to think the soul was a metaphor. Now I know there is a God—my God, in here, demanding not faith but experience, an inexhaustible wonder at the richness of this very moment.

COMPUTER CHIP FAITH

Whereas many adopt Kaplan's all-gods-are-my-god creed, not all are so satisfied with that eclectic theology. The current ambivalence toward faith has a history. During the roaringest of decades, the 1920s, mainstream America wanted to be seen sitting in church on Sunday mornings. The 1950s marked the end of a benevolent era of white, Protestant, upper-middle-class moral tranquillity, symbolized by the Eisenhower image.

Religiosity without substance crumbled beneath the upheaval and revolutions of the 1960s. The philosophy of Nietzsche and nihilism replaced morally bankrupt pseudo-faith. The 1960s generation of young adults was the product of 250 years of Enlightenment devotion to the mind, a century of skeptical Christianity, and a childhood centered in materialism mixed with fear of cold war nuclear disaster. Many rejected it all: "Enough pretense. I will make my own way bravely through a world in which God is irrelevant and life is hopeless. There is no truth beyond my truth now. Let's turn on to marijuana and drop out of social convention."

These first shock waves overtured an invasive earthquake of values and ideals in the 1970s. While the flower children were drifting into adulthood's realities and many returned to faith of one sort or another, their children were ill-equipped to believe in, or to take responsibility for, anything. God's irrelevance was joined by the nuclear family's predicted demise.

As the larger world seemed bent on self-destruction in the 1980s, Westerners turned cynical, isolationist, and self-absorbed. The idealist 1960s had become the materialist 1980s. Who was really shocked when financial and sexual scandals rocked high-profile religion? "Everybody's got an angle. Nobody really believes that stuff anymore." In God's providence, world power structures in the Middle East and Eastern Europe picked this moment to collapse. People all over the world hungered for faith with content, an answer to irrationality.

On the threshold of a new millennium, Kaplan speaks for those turned off by religions, skeptical about truth-claims, fearful without faith, and hungry for hope. The religion of the decade seems to be found in the computer chip and revivals of mysticism—the celebration of irrationality in search of "inexhaustible wonder," momentary virtual reality. Today practically every religion is respected and approved—*except* religion that speaks of absolute truth and narrow roads of obedience. The days of sentimental faith are over. A foreboding atmosphere hovers over culture. In this atmosphere, humanity looks to the future, not with breathless anticipation and enthusiasm, but with a sense of helplessness. What is needed is faith with muscles, solid truth to face the future. But content-filled truth is the only kind of truth that is utterly rejected. It is almost as if Paul had time-warped to the faith and morality of our society when he wrote Romans 1:22–24:

> Although they claimed to be wise, they became fools and exchanged the glory of the immortal God for images made to look like mortal man and birds and animals and reptiles. Therefore God gave them over in the sinful desires of their hearts to sexual impurity for the degrading of their bodies with one another. They exchanged the truth of God for a lie, and worshiped and served created things rather than the Creator—who is forever praised.

MEETING OF THE MIND, WILL, AND EMOTIONS

In this day of irrational, computer chip faith, belief with conviction is regarded as both dangerous bigotry and a fanciful flight into make-believe. The first charge, that believers are soul terrorists, will be addressed when we consider whether many flavors of truth can coexist. The second needs a response in defense of "I believe . . ." faith. Is faith merely a leap into the absurd, a flight from reality, an exercise in outmoded religion? Some Christians teach and live as if it is. But the authentic confession, "I believe . . . ," repudiates the absurd and the occult. Biblical Christianity knows nothing of blind leaps. Blindness, in biblical categories, marks the unbelieving mind. Faith in the New Testament sense begins as a thinking response to a divine summons and activity.

The New Testament picture of faith breaks out three dimensions as critical in distinguishing true Christian confession from other varieties of faith. These are the three dimensions to renewing your mind through faith: (1) faith has an intellectual dimension; (2) faith touches the human will profoundly; (3) faith is intimately bound to our emotions.

Faith and the Mind

History's Kaplans have always proclaimed faith to be basically nonrational, an affair of the heart but not of the mind. Around the year 200, an influential Christian teacher named Tertullian propounded the idea that it is noble to believe something that is absurd. In fact, a certain courage is required to reject what everyone else considers rational and to believe what seems absurd, but anyone who follows absurdity very far has more valor than discretion. Tertullian is like contemporary thinkers who call us to blind faith in the midst of meaninglessness. Yet this noble faith is far removed from what the Bible describes. Here is no invitation to embrace contradiction. Certainly we do have to believe propositions we don't always totally understand. But the same is true of all modern life. Otherwise, most of us couldn't use the sophisticated gadgetry that technology now provides. In the realm of the supernatural, mysteries that stretch far beyond the reach of the mind are hinted at in creation and described in Scripture. But such mysteries are coherent and mutually compatible. If God seems to be calling evil good or green red, we had better study further to see what we have wrong. Incoherence is never the mark of God. We become confused; God's Holy Spirit does not.

This distinctive of the Christian faith is crucial. Valid truth is the faith to bear us through a crisis. We need not clench our fists, grit our teeth, and believe something is irrational in order to salve over our feelings of hopelessness. The Christian draws faith muscle from Jesus' rational proposition and comfort:

In this world you will have trouble. But take heart! I have overcome the world. (John 16:33b)

Jesus makes an absolute truth-claim: "I have overcome the world." As we learn to trust that claim as truth and grasp the fullness of what Jesus means, we strengthen our belief muscles. We can actually participate in Christ's victory. It would be irrational *not* to take heart.

To say that faith is reasonable is not to confuse faith with rationalism. Rationalism emphasizes the mind's ability to understand all reality without help. A young wife lies in an intensive care unit and must be told that her husband and child did not survive the car accident. Sharing her grief, we can only admit our incomprehension and say, "God, we don't understand, but we accept that you do understand and are trustworthy."

It is at this point that Kaplan's belief in relative truth seems most dissatisfying. *Truth is truth, whether it ever touches my understanding.* Even if I don't understand the truth or know what it is, why should I mystically trust both Buddha and Jesus? They are saying diametrically opposed things; they cannot both be true. I much prefer the path of understanding, imperfect as it is, so that true truth is able to touch my life.

Because faith does not exist in a vacuum of understanding, Christians need credal statements that summarize the connection between thinking and acting faith. The Christian confessing the Apostles' Creed begins with the statement "I believe." Then the believer goes on to summarize in broad strokes the extent of that belief. The Holy Spirit does not call us to faith in general, but to faith in particular—to faith in the person and work of Jesus Christ.

If, as Romans 3:20–28 and other passages teach, a person is justified by faith alone, this question of understanding is vital. Christian leaders of the sixteenth-century Reformation understood this. They carefully defined what is needed for faith to be saving faith, for faith in Jesus to be declared righteousness before God: *content, intellectual assent,* and *personal trust.*

Content is the information communicated by the Bible. This content includes the facts that God exists, that he entered history in the God-man Jesus Christ, and that in Christ's death, resurrection, and ascension we have eternal life. To be a believer one must understand who Jesus is and what he is all about.

A believer must not only be aware of the content, however, but must also give *intellectual assent.* To be a Christian, I must know that Jesus died on the cross and then believe that his act is sufficient to pay the penalty for my sins and bridge the chasm between me and the Father. My mind must regard as true the content of the faith if I am to be truly a believer. That brings us to the central issue of *trust.*

Faith and the Will

What if I have all the content straight and clearly understand it in my mind and am willing to acknowledge that all of this is indeed true? Does that give me saving faith? Not according to the Bible. Luke records that the first beings to recognize the true identity of Jesus were not faithful disciples. Demons penetrated his disguise and recognized instantly that he was the Son of the most high God.[2] Although they recognize the truth about God, they hate that truth. The apostle James uses this point to distinguish between dead faith and vital faith. Here sarcasm drips from the apostle's pen:

> You believe that there is one God. Good! Even the demons believe that— and shudder. You foolish man, do you want evidence that faith without deeds is useless? (James 2:19–20)

To give intellectual assent to the things of God only elevates a person from the status of pagan to the level of the demon. It advances the soul not a centimeter into the kingdom of God. Satan assents to the facts, but does not possess saving faith. The New Testament teaches that the individual must act upon the content.

If this were an open dialogue among divergent Christian theologies, a number of hands would by now be raised in an effort to get the floor. The representatives of one group would say that our formulation of will and faith slides much too far to the side of will. "Don't you know that the will has nothing to do with faith? No one comes to Christ in true belief unless compelled by the Holy Spirit." The second part of the statement is true: A sinful human being is every bit as much a rebel against Christ as a demon. We shall see later why the hardened heart requires a supernatural work of God to be able to confess with a willing heart, "I believe." On the other hand, a willing heart is, in fact, *willing*. Believing and obeying are acts in which I take part. I am willing or salvation never happens. God intervenes or I am never willing.

Activist Christians will next raise their voices to tell me that I am missing an important point. Their slogan is that "Faith is a verb, not a noun." "It is more important to do faith through loving God and serving others than to cogitate in a theological ivory tower and formulate creeds."

Once again, partly true. For faith to be real, I must apply my faith to my personal situation. But do not be led into a false dichotomy: The Bible welds my acts of obedience to the content of my confession. A multitude of churches and individual believers have been drawn by this polarity to do great acts of charity while teaching a little god that is totally foreign to the God of Scripture. Some have gone so far as to reject the elemental truth and meaning of Jesus' birth, death, resurrection, ascension, and lordship. Philanthropy is not enough; doing is never the sum of faith.

Faith and the Emotions

Meaningful faith has content; it involves the mind in a serious way. One more, personal aspect remains, which we can broadly call "love." Love is the inclination of affections or the disposition of the heart toward Christ. Love, however, is too broad a term; we need to hone its use in describing our attitude toward God.

The psalmist said the righteous person's "delight" focuses on God.[3] The godly heart delights in the things of God, joyfully embracing God's sovereign rule. The ungodly person, by contrast, is characterized throughout Scripture by personal estrangement and hostility. Quoting Isaiah 29:13, Jesus remarked, "These people honor me with their lips, but their hearts are far from me" (Matt. 15:8). People of faith set their heart affections on God. They pursue, they seek, they press into the kingdom. Those without true faith remain indifferent, aloof, or hostile. Therefore, faith is more than persuasion of truth. Faith loves truth. Faith delights in Christ. Faith—true faith—loves to lift Christ in praise.

HANDLE GROWING FAITH WITH CARE

"I believe . . ." faith trains spiritual muscle through content, will, and emotions. It renews the mind, helping the believer to stand and to discern truth in the midst of a hostile world. Fantasies and compromise with worldly philosophy have always demanded a honed faith. Each age of church history has had its own problems with superstition and error. Quite a number are floating around today, and two of them are particularly relevant to our introduction to belief. Strong faith understands what God has really promised about our lives in a troubled world as well as where faith and works properly meet in Christian living.

Faith and Superstition

Some well-meaning persons confuse biblical faith with elements of superstition. Their wrong-headed teachings seriously damage the faith of new Christians, who are invariably let down by false promises. Some preachers maintain, in one form or another, "Come to Jesus. God will lift all of your burdens. You need never be troubled again." What troubled person wouldn't respond to a gospel like this? Because it is not the real gospel, however, misled converts often become bitter and disappointed. Some mature and learn from the experience; others abandon Christianity altogether. Most limp along, wondering why their faith doesn't quite cut it with God.

Fact: Life is never so complicated as when we embark on the pilgrimage and discover that this game is being played for keeps. Ethical issues weigh heavy on a newly sensitized conscience. Weakness and ongoing battles with sin should be over, shouldn't they? They certainly are not.

Now add to those stresses the pressure of being told:

> "Your sickness is of the devil. God wants to cast it out right now. All he requires is my hands as a channel for healing power and your unquestioning faith."

> "God did not make his children to suffer but to prosper. The faith to move mountains will give you every desire of your heart if you ask, *believing.*"

> "You have the authority to bind Satan's power in your boss/parent/child/spouse. Do so in faith, and you will never be harmed by this person again."

Healing and prosperity are not God's purposes in "I believe . . ." faith. They are not God's promises. In fact, the Bible promises over and over that Christians will suffer many things. Suffering allows us to share in the humiliation and suffering of our Lord; pain makes us more effective witnesses and more mature lovers of God, dependent on him for strength. Shattered people led astray by false promises and specious Bible interpretation are denied these benefits. They must discover that, in spite of their faith, they share space with the lost at the emergency room and funeral home. They are not abandoned by God, but neither are they immune from tragic disease and lost prosperity.

Superstition robs faith of its muscle. Superstition sugarcoats the call to suffering that is a part of the gospel of Christ. Superstition cheapens the cost of discipleship. True faith calls for discipline, for courage, for endurance, for growth, in order that we may face with triumph the difficulties that surround us in the pilgrimage of life.

Faith and Works

The Epistle of James differentiates living faith from dead faith. This difference is really one between true faith and false faith, for dead/false faith is no faith at all. True faith, always and without exception, produces works, the test of obedience. James (2:21–23) cites Abraham's response to God's command to sacrifice his beloved son Isaac as a model of true faith (Gen. 22). Abraham is vindicated as his actions show his faith. This does not mean that good works necessarily mean saving faith is present. It means that where true faith is present, good works inevitably and immediately follow. Without obedience, salvation is demonstrably absent. Jesus stated it like this in John 14:15: "If you love me, you will obey what I command."

Fidelity is a word that has fallen into disuse, but it well represents what is required. Many banks once incorporated under the name Fidelity Bank and Trust. The bank directors promised to be faithful stewards of the money entrusted to them. Their propriety would be trustworthy. What we do in obedience to Christ shows our fidelity. Our lives are to be characterized by commandment-keeping. Through a long process of maturing, we conform more and more to the will of Christ. The life of Jesus is the New Testament model of fidelity. Saints of the Old Testament, such as Abraham, Moses, and Elijah, are examples of faith, but these heroes are dwarfed by Jesus' standard of fidelity to the Father. "My food," said Jesus, "is to do the will of him who sent me and to finish his work" (John 4:34).

Faith involves *confessing* more than *professing;* in the final analysis, it is a platform of commitment to the will of God. Faith's content fills the mind and grasps the heart to the end that new life is apparent.

FAITH AND CONFESSIONS OF FAITH

The church uses credal statements and confessional formulas to articulate the content of its faith. Yesterday's creed, however, may become today's museum piece; the language becomes dated. There is one confession, the Apostles' Creed, which has endured time and battles over belief more successfully than any other.

Despite its name, none of the words come from the original apostles. In its present form it has been in continual use since about A.D. 700, but elements of its wording have been traced to a baptismal confession from early-second-century Rome. The Apostles' Creed remains a simple, succinct, and clear affirmation of "I believe . . ." faith. The following chapters offer a contemporary explanation of its teaching—not to give a historical exposition of each point, but to apply its basic tenets to contemporary faith-issues.

If the church is to be the church, with members renewed in mind and growing in spiritual maturity, the content of this statement of faith remains crucial, because as Christians we believe.

RELATED RESOURCES FROM LIGONIER MINISTRIES

John H. Gerstner. "Handout Theology: Salvation," video or audio series.
———. *Reasons for Faith.*
———. "The Westminster Confession of Faith," video or audio series.
Matthew Mead. *The Almost Christian Discovered.*

R. C. Sproul. "Born Again," video or audio series and leader's guide and study guide.

———. Developing Godly Character," video or audio series.

———. *Essential Truths of the Christian Faith.*

———. *Faith Alone: The Evangelical Doctrine of Justification.*

———. "Heroes of the Christian Faith," audio series.

———. "Objections Answered," video series.

———. "Repentance," audio series.

———. *The Soul's Quest for God.*

———. "Truth," audio series.

———, ed. *Doubt and Assurance.*

The Puritans on Conversion.

"Themes in Apologetics," audio series.

I believe in God.

God-talk

hat is the most important question that someone in today's society needs to have answered?"

I didn't have to ponder the question posed by a businessman.

"That's easy. The most important thing for modern secular people to understand is who God is."

"Not *whether* God is?"

"No, the critical issue is God's identity. God's existence is not obscured today, but his nature and personality certainly are."

He had another question.

"Well, what do you think is the most important question that *Christians* need to have answered?"

"That's easy, too. The most important thing for modern Christians to understand is who God is."

That stopped my friend in his tracks.

"But a person can't even *be* a Christian without having some idea of who God is. Right?"

No one can come to Christ without having *some* knowledge of who God is. But after one comes to Christ, the issue is whether knowledge grows or stays puny and vague. Unfortunately, a flea could wade in the depth of knowledge about God in the mind of the average Christian. That is too shallow a level for a meaningful, growing relationship. There is a famine in the knowledge of God in general and the knowledge of God the Father in particular. Many books are being written about the person and work of Christ. Many more have appeared, especially in recent years, on the person and work of the Holy Spirit. The quality of some of these books is questionable or worse, but the market indicates that people are definitely interested in knowing Jesus and the Holy Spirit. The Christian must understand Jesus and the Holy Spirit. But Jesus and the Holy Spirit are sent from the Father. One of their tasks is to reveal to us the nature of the Father. They haven't found much cooperation for that task in the church.

"I believe in God . . ."

One woman told me that her deepest desire is to be brought into the presence of God in worship—to have her vision of God extended. But, she went on, it seems that God is being hidden from her instead. Worshiping with others in her church, God becomes obscured rather than revealed. She said, "Sometimes I wonder if preachers do that on purpose so as not to confront us with some of the frightening or demanding aspects of the nature of God." Whatever the reason, the absence of the knowledge of God was breaking her heart. She had a passionate desire to know God in a more personal, dynamic way. Every Christian must know who God is if he or she is to grow in personal worship and obedience.

In the midst of his popularity after the "Million Man March" in 1996, Louis Farrakhan was the center of a disturbing picture at one of his rallies. No one expects Minister Farrakhan of the Nation of Islam to know any other god than Allah or to represent a Christian perspective of any sort. So what was wrong with this picture? Farrakhan preached to a large, packed auditorium, surrounded on the platform by Christian ministers. Some of them lead large urban churches. With all his oratorical skill, Farrakhan was letting them have it. He corrected their theology. He told them about who Jesus *really* was. He told them to get with God's program. They just sat there and took it. Some were caught up in the moment, echoed in their "amens" and enthusiastic applause.

So does our view of God have content? If Christian beliefs can coexist in the same philosophical universe with Farrakhan's racially pure, New Age Islam, we have to wonder whether it is possible to say anything meaningful about God at all. Farrakhan believes Jesus was one prophet of Allah, and that the God of the universe has a special plan of salvation for his special (nonwhite-only) people. He has sent huge space ships to hover over major cities and quietly beam up the seed of a new Eden before the final race war destroys earth. Now *that's* content! Louis Farrakhan has something definite in mind when he refers to God. He believes in a spiritual reality that exists apart from himself. By all rights he should not have been able to find Christians willing to share a dais with him, let alone give him an "amen."

So what is it with these cowed preachers at Farrakhan's command? Unfortunately, their God doesn't lack content—he lacks *biblical* content. So their theology is a hodgepodge based on what works and whose bandwagon happens to be rolling by. They are children of nineteenth-century philosophers who declared God to be unknowable and our concept of God to be simply an inner aspect of our own humanity. The true religion, said the next generation of reforming theologians, is to *become* Christ and to incarnate his kingdom through social action. They saw themselves as participants in a social evolution that would end when humanity became divinity. Some of their European cousins poured similar social evolution ideas into a pot of Nietzsche and cooked up a little national socialism. Others stirred the same ingredients into a theoretical economic mold and served up Marxist socialism. Add existentialism and you have the "God is dead" movement of the 1960s and the feminist goddess worship and "Jesus Seminar" so popular in the mid-1990s. This is not to oversimplify the philosophy and theology articulated over the past couple of centuries. It is to say that when there is an absence of the knowledge of God—even in those who identify themselves as Christians and theologians—disaster waits in the wings for a cue.

GOD AND ICE CREAM CONES

A simple experiment can sharpen our understanding of the problem of having content about God and communicating it meaningfully to those around us. I've used it on people of all ages and levels of theological sophistication, and the results varied little.

Ready?

Close your eyes and think in concrete images about a two-dip cone of your favorite icecream flavor.

What flavor are you visualizing? The answers vary from pistachio nut to raspberry ripple. In a large group, the summary looks like the flavor menu at an icecream specialty outlet. We have little trouble contemplating icecream cones in concrete terms.

Close your eyes again. This time think in concrete images about God—not God the Son, not God the Holy Spirit, but God the Father.

A little tougher? Some people respond by saying they visualize "love." The concept *love* is as abstract as the concept *God* and gives us little concrete insight into what or who God is. These people mean that the word *God* evokes positive feelings similar to feelings evoked by the word *love*. This association reveals something of our personal relationship with God, but adds little to concrete imagination. With a little effort, though, most people can conjure up a mental image for the word *God*. A child's images differ little from those of a theological scholar. The images may be of an old man with a beard on a white throne or Michelangelo's God of creation on the ceiling of the Sistine Chapel. The image may be a cloud of gray smoke, a red button on a massive instrument panel, a beloved family member, a volcanic eruption; a nuclear explosion, a lightning flash across a black sky, a brilliant white light, or a giant brain.

Now answer a question: Do you think God is a cloud of smoke, a volcanic eruption, or a giant brain? Every time I've asked the question, the response has been unanimous. Of course not! God cannot be absolutely identified with any of these images. But the ideas still communicate something concrete *about* God. They help pour substance into the term *God*, which is hazy and ambiguous, yet still meaningful.

Analyze the images mentioned above and others you may have come up with. Each concept is similar to the others. All describe God in common, familiar human terms. All help us think of God *analogically*. God is in some way *like* the white light or the red button, though God extends far beyond the likeness of the analogy. The Bible's references to God also take advantage of human, analogous images.

SPEAKING OF GOD

The Christian philosopher and theologian Thomas Aquinas (1224–74) differentiated three descriptive uses of language. *Univocal* use of language applies a single descriptive term to different things, showing that they are basically the same. For example, the word *bald*, applied to men and to eagles, means substantially the same thing. The phrase, "the man is bald," means the same thing as the phrase, "the eagle is bald." The term *bald* in either case means the absence of hair (or feathers) on the head. The bald eagle, of course, does have feathers on its head; they are simply white and reminded whoever named the bird of a bald head. So, to share the perception with the rest of the eagle watchers, univocal language was used. Upon hearing the term and seeing the bird, the mind instantly goes through some mental gymnastics. "Bald means no hair. . . . Eagle has feathers. . . . Ah, but white feathers on dark bird look like no feathers. Gotcha." Univocal language is good for drawing a subtle analogy between two very different levels of being. The term's meaning remains relatively stable. It simply adapts to fit what is currently being described.

The *equivocal* use of language is that use where the meaning of a term changes radically when applied to two different orders of reality. (Equivocation is a common cause of logical fallacies.) For example, suppose a college student attended a dramatic reading program, and, upon his return to his dormitory, he told his roommate it was a "bald" narrative. What would he mean? Would he mean that the narrative didn't have hair on its head? Obviously not, as a narrative has neither head nor hair (some contemporary plays notwithstanding). Does this mean, then, that the term *bald* when applied to a narrative is utterly meaningless? No. In the equivocal use of the term *bald* in this case, there remains a point of contact with physical baldness, as remote as that contact may be. What the student was saying was that something was *lacking* in the narrative. Probably it was very dull and unexciting, and, as a bald man lacks hair, so the narrative lacked dynamic punch. Hence, equivocal language is that language where the meaning of the term changes radically when applied to two different realms.

Aquinas maintained that we cannot use univocal language to communicate accurate content about God. The differences between creature and Creator are so profound that attempts to use theological vocabulary to describe an order of being so unlike any created thing is hopeless. Theologically speaking, God is transcendentally "other." His ways are not our ways. Theologians call this the *Deus absconditus* (the "hidden aspect of God"). But

Aquinas warns us not to use equivocal language either. The confession "Jesus is the Son of God" can have an enormous range of meaning, depending on how the word *son* is defined. If I stood next to a Mormon and we repeated that sentence in unison the meanings we attach to the words are totally different. It isn't enough to let words mean anything or nothing, just because they refer to the *Deus absconditus*. Univocal language assumes too much similarity between God and man; equivocal language assumes too little.

For Aquinas, the most meaningful God-talk is *analogical*. Analogical language uses terms whose meanings change with what is being described. We speak of a *good* man and a *good* dog. A good dog is obedient and does not bite. A good man does not go around biting people, but the reason we describe him in terms of "goodness" obviously does not refer to that fact. Yet the meaning is not so far removed as to be called equivocal. The term *good*, when applied to dogs and people, has a greater point of contact than do the meanings for the word *bald* as it can refer a narrative. Analogical language is less meaningful than univocal language, but it bows to the *Deus absconditus* and the *Deus revelatus* aspects of God. It does not provide exhaustive comprehension of God, but neither does it leave us in hopeless ignorance. Aquinas looked to analogical language as a meaningful way to talk about God. It is possible because the *Deus revelatus* has pasted some snapshot likenesses of himself on creation and history.

The Way of Negation

Because we are unable to describe God univocally, some have argued that we cannot say anything positive about God even analogically. All we can say about God is what he is not. The classic proponent of such a negative view was the Neo-Platonist philosopher, Plotinus. For Plotinus, God, or "The One," is totally unknowable except by mystical experience that gives no rationally communicable content:

He that would speak exactly must not name it by this name or by that; we can but circle, as it were, about its circumference, seeking to interpret in speech our experience of it, now shooting near the mark, and again disappointed of our aim by reason of the antinomies we find in it.[1]

It was the incomprehensibility of God that occupied much of Melville's reflection in *Moby Dick*. The awe-inspiring "whiteness" of the whale manifested the ambiguity of God. Ishmael wondered:

Is it that by its indefiniteness it shadows forth the heartless voids and immensities of the universe, and thus stabs us from behind with the thought of annihilation, when beholding the white depths of the milky way? Or is it, that as in essence whiteness is not so much a color as the visible absence of color, and at the same time the concrete of all colors; is it for these reasons that there is such a dumb blankness, full of meaning, in a wide landscape of snows—a colorless, all-color of atheism from which we shrink? . . . Pondering all this, the palsied universe lies before us a leper; and like wilful travelers in Lapland, who refuse to wear colored and coloring glasses upon their eyes, so the wretched infidel gazes himself blind at the monumental white shroud that wraps all the prospect around him. And of all these things the Albino whale was the symbol. Wonder ye then at the fiery hunt?[2]

Negation keeps us from assuming that we know more about God than we actually do. It reminds us of the *Deus absconditus* (the hidden aspect of God). It prohibits us from giving univocal import or analogical descriptions. It emphasizes that "my thoughts are not your thoughts, neither are your ways my ways. . . . As the heavens are higher than the earth, so are my ways higher than your ways and my thoughts than your thoughts" (Isa. 55:8–9). With David we cry, "Such knowledge is too wonderful for me, too lofty for me to attain" (Ps. 139:6).

The Way of Affirmation

Negation may serve as a necessary balance, but it is not the primary way for the Christian. The believer is not left in a dismal abyss of total darkness. There is no place in the Christian church for a monument TO AN UNKNOWN GOD (Acts 17:23). To reduce Christianity to total negation is to side with the fool. Luther stated with boldness:

> To take no pleasure in assertions is not the mark of a Christian heart; indeed, one must delight in assertions to be a Christian at all. . . . Away, now, with Sceptics and Academics from the company of us Christians; let us have men who will assert, men twice as inflexible as very Stoics! . . . Nothing is more familiar or characteristic among Christians than assertion. Take away assertions, and you take away Christianity. . . . The Holy Spirit is no Sceptic, and the things he has written in our hearts are not doubts or opinions, but assertions—surer and more certain than sense and life itself.[3]

To deny what we do know on the basis of what we do not know is not only bad theology but also bad science. A one-sided emphasis on the *Deus absconditus* fails to do justice to the *Deus revelatus* (that aspect of God that is revealed). So the church has proclaimed and confessed that knowledge of God is not only possible, but that God can be adequately known and described.

NAMING GOD

One of the most significant ways of speaking about God is by means of his name. The third commandment of the Decalogue prohibits the desecration of the name of God. The first petition of the Lord's Prayer is that the name of God be hallowed. There is a unique and inseparable connection between God and his name. To use the name of God flippantly or as a curse word is to manifest blatant disrespect for God. The Jews' reticence to utter the ineffable name did not arise out of a superstitious view that a name projected magical power, but rather out of holy respect for the God bearing that name. God's name is holy because he is holy (Lev. 11:44–45).

What's in a Name?

The close relationship between person and name that is found throughout the Bible is not entirely foreign to us. A college student entered class one morning, obviously delighted and enthused. A diamond ring on her left hand and her dreamy gaze toward the young man seated beside her made the reason for her delight abundantly obvious. I put her on the spot by asking, "Mary, did you just get engaged?"

When she answered in the affirmative, I said, "Would you mind if I inferred from the fact that you are engaged to John that you are also in love with John?"

She agreed.

"Why do you love John?"

She responded enthusiastically that he was handsome.

I pointed to Bill, who recently had been elected escort to the campus queen, and asked Mary if she also thought Bill was handsome. Yes, she did. There must, then, be something else.

She was quick to add that John was athletic. Bill sat in the back of the room wearing a varsity sweater adorned with letters in three major sports. When I called Mary's attention to that, she hastily added that John was intelligent. But Bill was president of the academic honor society.

Showing frustration, Mary singled out John's propensity for courtesy. I asked Mary, "Are you suggesting that Bill is rude?" By this time the class was hysterical and thoroughly enjoying Mary's rising level of frustration. To spare Mary further discomfort, I asked her to name precisely and definitively the quality that most attracted her to John.

"I love him because he's . . . because he's . . . because, uh . . . because he's *John*." Instantly, the class realized what had happened: When Mary failed to capture the uniqueness of John in his attributes, she resorted ultimately to his name. The name *John* meant to Mary, not a word on a birth certificate, but the symbol of all that he was and the whole history of their relationship.

Christian faith does not involve belief in God-in-general. The Christian is not a theist whose hope rests in a "supreme being," but a Yahwist whose hope rests in the God and Father of our Lord Jesus Christ. God is revealed to us in concrete acts of history. The one who revealed himself to Moses gave "I AM WHO I AM" as a name, not a definition (Exod. 3:14). Emil Brunner points out that "the Name of God is only a 'proper Name' because it does not stand alongside of a general conception, of an appellation. The plural 'gods' is an insult to God; it belongs to the Nature of God that there should be none other beside Him."[4]

Thus, the God of Scripture is the God of Abraham, Isaac, and Jacob. He is the God who brought Israel out of bondage. He reveals himself through redemptive history. God also manifests himself in and through his creation. The psalmist says, "The heavens declare the glory of God; the skies proclaim the work of his hands" (Ps. 19:1). Paul maintained that "since the creation of the world God's invisible qualities—his eternal power and divine nature—have been clearly seen, being understood from what has been made, so that men are without excuse" (Rom. 1:20).

The Father Revealed in the Son

God is known generally in creation and specifically in the events of redemptive history. God is not known, however, simply in the naked events of this history. He does not just work and leave it up to us to somehow discover who is working and what is being said in the event. God not only acts; he speaks through his prophets and apostles. The Scriptures are the normative source of special revelation because they provide not only a record of God's acts, but also an inspired interpretation of those acts. It is because of this quality of Scripture that Jesus called the prophets and the apostles the foundation of the church. Any attempt to isolate the biblical record of events from the biblical interpretation of those events must lead to despair. Such a separation leaves us with chameleon events that change color with every fantasy of the interpreter.

The zenith of God's self-revelation is the person and work of Christ, the "Logos," who is also called "the radiance of God's glory and the exact representation of his being, sustaining all things by his powerful word" (Heb. 1:3). God's supreme revelation of himself is the incarnation, the Word becoming flesh and speaking to us at our level of understanding. It was Philip who said to Jesus, "Lord, show us the Father and that will be enough for us." If ever a note of impatience or frustration crept into Jesus' voice, it is in his reply to Philip's request. "Don't you know me, Philip, even after I have been among you such a long time? Anyone who has seen me has seen the Father. How can you say, 'Show us the Father'?" (John 14:8–10). The staggering statement, "Anyone who has seen me has seen the Father," forms the ground for all Christian talk about God. It is the incarnation that drives the Christian from the way of negation to the way of affirmation.

CONCRETE AND ABSTRACT LANGUAGE

Many attempts have been made throughout history to sharpen and refine our language of God in order to transcend the barrier posed in the tension between the *Deus absconditus* and the *Deus revelatus*. Philosophical terms can help the scholar, but often confuse univocal and analogical language. We have often thought to penetrate the essence of God by abstract language. Some have sought a "God beyond God" to escape the dilemma. Unfortunately, there is no God beyond God, and to attempt to transcend the analogical limits of human speech requires that we first transcend our own humanity. All of our language is anthropomorphic because we are all *anthropoi* ("human"). All human talk of God must be rejected if we attach univocal weight to it, but it is not necessary to speak univocally to speak meaningfully.

Helmut Gollwitzer has properly stated that particular and concrete ways of speaking are better than general and abstract ones; moreover, personal ways of speaking are preferable to impersonal, neutral ones.[5] To speak with concrete and simple images makes it obvious that our images are not to be taken univocally. When God asks Moses, "Is the LORD's arm too short?" (Num. 11:23), he is asking, in effect, "Moses, are you dealing with a divine cripple? Do I have a withered arm?" Here God speaks clearly and graphically of his overwhelming power. The "arm of the Lord" is a frequent image in the Bible that communicates simply, but meaningfully.

When God says that "every animal of the forest is mine, and the cattle on a thousand hills" (Ps. 50:10), we are clearly not being told that God is the Great Rancher in the Sky who occasionally has a shoot-out with Satan at the O.K. Corral. Rather, we are being told that God claims ownership over his creation and that we are to bow to his authority. The simpler and more concrete the image, the less likely the confusion.

We confess, "I believe in God." That confession is not an expression of a creative imagination or an instance of projection, but a response to the One who manifests himself in creation, in history, in deed and in word, and, supremely, in Christ. Our talk of him is legitimate because he has entered into the arena of human activity. We confess not only that there is a God, but that God can be known and that our knowledge of him can be meaningfully communicated.

RELATED RESOURCES
FROM LIGONIER MINISTRIES

John Gerstner. "Handout Theology: Natural Revelation; Supernatural Revelation; Trinity, Decrees, Creation, and Providence," video or audio series.

————. *Theology in Dialogue.*

R. C. Sproul. "Contemporary Theology," audio series.

————. "God's Law and the Christian," audio series.

————. "Hath God Said?" video or audio series.

————. "If There Is a God, Why Are There Atheists?" video or audio.

————. "Knowing God's Will," audio series.

————. "Knowing Scripture," video or audio series or book.

————. "The History of Christian Theology," audio series.

————. "The History of Philosophy," audio series.

————. "Themes from Deuteronomy," audio series.

————. "What Is Truth?" video or audio.

————, and John Gerstner. "Silencing the Devil," video or audio series and study guide.

————, et al. *Sola Scriptura.*

Oletta Wald. *The Joy of Discovery in Bible Study.*

I believe in God
the Father Almighty.

3

Spiritual Genetics

The fatherhood of God has been a source of much controversy in the Christian church. In eighteenth-century America, Unitarianism emerged as an alternative to classical Christianity. At the heart of the Unitarian creed was the ideal of the universal fatherhood of God and the brotherhood of all humanity. The same universal fatherhood was an integral part of nineteenth-century liberal Christianity. The growth of anthropological studies encouraged the development of a "science of comparative religion," which sought to distill the essence of universal belief from various world religions. With such a basic common denominator, the religions might be able to unite, at least conceptually. If it could be shown that God was the Father of all humanity, then it would follow that all people are brothers and sisters, and no one could claim exclusive knowledge of or privilege from the Father.

God's fatherhood was a component of the counterculture church of the 1960s and 1970s, which looked for the religious equivalent of the Age of Aquarius. A couple songs summarized the mood. "Let Peace Begin on Earth" had as part of its refrain:

> With God as our Father,
>> Brothers all are we;
> Let me walk with my brother
>> In perfect harmony.

Lyrics to another song, "One God," were even more explicit:

> So many people calling on him
> By many a-diff-rent name.
> One Father, loving each the same.

Such unity under the Father sounds so right, but is so wrong, for it doesn't correspond to the realities of the holiness of God or the human condition.

CHILDREN OF ABRAHAM, CHILDREN OF WRATH

The New Testament speaks of God as Father in two ways. In a broad sense, God is the Father of all creation. Paul, at Mars Hill, alludes to the universal fatherhood of God when he says:

> From one man he made every nation of men, that they should inhabit the whole earth; and he determined the times set for them and the exact places where they should live. God did this so that men would seek him and perhaps reach out for him and find him, though he is not far from each one of us. "For in him we live and move and have our being." As some of your own poets have said, "We are his offspring." (Acts 17:26–28)

> I Believe in God, the Father Almighty . . .

Paul acknowledges that all human beings are "offspring" of God in the sense that we are all dependent on God for our origin and continuing existence. As Creator, God is the ultimate progenitor. Also, God gives his common grace liberally. His rain falls on the just as well as on the unjust (Matt. 5:45).

However, the Bible says that to call on God as Father involves far more than acknowledging his powers of creation or his control over the universe. Primarily, it refers to a personal filial relationship that is not assumed outside a relationship with Christ. The question of sonship and fatherhood was a critical and stormy issue for Jesus and his contemporaries. To escape the indictment Jesus levied against their bondage to sin, the Jews appealed to their relationship with the patriarchs. God had given Abraham his covenant promises. Jesus' contemporaries claimed, "Abraham is our father."

But Jesus replied,

> "If you were Abraham's children," said Jesus, "then you would do the things Abraham did. As it is, you are determined to kill me, a man who has told you the truth that I heard from God. Abraham did not do such things. You are doing the things your own father does."
> "We are not illegitimate children," they protested. "The only Father we have is God himself."
> Jesus said to them, "If God were your Father, you would love me, for I came from God and now am here. I have not come on my own; but he sent me. Why is my language not clear to you? Because you are unable to hear what I say." (John 8:39–44)

Jesus clearly denies a universal inside track with God. Sonship is inseparably related to obedience. We are the children of those whom we love and serve. To honor the Father is to honor the Son. To claim God as Father and at the same time disavow the Son is to miss the entire point of biblical fatherhood. Jesus said, "He who does not honor the Son does not honor the Father, who sent him" (John 5:23). That narrow exclusiveness was a scandal to the Jews and it is a scandal yet today. The Bible does not define sonship in biological terms. There is a clearly implied spiritual distinction between the "children of light" and the "children of darkness." We are not born the children of God. It was Israel's grave error to assume automatic filial relationship with God on the basis of genealogy. Sonship comes through faith, not genetics. "We were," says Paul, "by nature children of wrath" (Eph. 2:3 KJV).

SPIRITUAL SONS AND DAUGHTERS

Nicodemus was bewildered. A spiritual leader of the Jewish people, he saw in Jesus a dimension of knowledge about God that he and his colleagues in the Sanhedrin lacked. Now at night, by the light of a dim Palestinian lamp in an obscure Jerusalem home, Nicodemus strained to read Jesus' expression. Was he serious? Was there hidden in Jesus' words about birth the news that Nicodemus lacked not only knowledge of God, but any connection with him at all? Jesus spoke:

> "I tell you the truth, no one can see the kingdom of God unless he is born again."
> "How can a man be born when he is old?" Nicodemus asked. "Surely he cannot enter a second time into his mother's womb to be born!"
> Jesus answered, "I tell you the truth, no one can enter the kingdom of God unless he is born of water and the Spirit. Flesh gives birth to flesh, but the Spirit gives birth to spirit." (John 3:3b–6)

Jesus relates sonship to a radical spiritual realignment, as radical as when a baby first emerges from a mother's womb—regeneration. Sonship is not automatic, but comes through the work of the Holy Spirit. "Yet to all who received him, to those who believed in his name, he gave the right to become children of God—children born not of natural descent, nor of human decision or a husband's will, but born of God" (John 1:12–13). This regeneration cannot be accomplished by human effort, heredity, or achievement. It is by the power of the Spirit that we become children of God. Perhaps this is most clearly seen in Paul's teaching regarding sonship in Romans 8:

> Those who are led by the Spirit of God are sons of God. For you did not receive a spirit that makes you a slave again to fear, but you received the Spirit of sonship. And by him we cry, "*Abba*, Father." The Spirit himself testifies with our spirit that we are God's children. Now if we are children,

then we are heirs—heirs of God and co-heirs with Christ, if indeed we share in his sufferings in order that we may also share in his glory. (vv. 14–17)

When Jesus instructs his disciples to address God in prayer as "Our Father," he is sharing a unique privilege with his friends. In the word *Father* is contained the history of God's paternal love and care for us. When we call on God as Father, we are not only giving God praise and honor, but we are acknowledging his authority over us.

That filial relationship is a powerful vertical connection between believers and God. Another powerful horizontal connection ties believers to one another. This is a strange new family tree. We are related to all other people in the world as neighbors, but brotherhood comes only through relationship to Christ.[1] Christ alone is the Son of God in the ultimate sense. He is the "only-begotten." But in him we are adopted into the family of God. We are brothers and sisters with all other adopted sons and daughters who are joined to Christ. We may be divided theologically. We may not even want to be spiritually related to some of these people. But if the same Spirit is shared by all, then brotherhood exists. We can't choose our spiritual relatives.

ALMIGHTY

God was known to the Israelites as the "Almighty One." That he was not simply "mighty," but "all"-mighty distinguished him from the spurious deities of the pagans. His power extends over all creation. He is not a storm-god, though the storm indeed is evidence of his awesome power. He is not a fertility-god, yet he is in control of seasonal changes. He is not a war-god like Mars, but no army can stand against him. He is *all*-mighty.

When God's attributes are catalogued, he is usually described as omniscient (all-knowing) and omnipotent (all-powerful). God's omnipotence has been the target of many budding theologians, who wanted to stump their professors with the supposedly unanswerable question:

"Can God build a rock so big that he is unable to move it?"

Sounds like a serious problem, doesn't it? If we answer affirmatively, we are protecting God's omnipotence with one hand while taking it away with the other, for there is something God cannot do, that is, move the rock. If we answer in the negative, we are still saying there is something God cannot do, namely, build the rock. Or there just might be an error in a basic assumption: that omnipotence means, univocally, that God can do anything. The word itself literally means "omni" ("all") and "potence" ("power or ability"). Here is an example of how abstract terms can lead us into theological hot water. The word *omnipotence* was never intended to suggest that God could do *everything*. The Scriptures speak forthrightly about certain things God cannot do. We are told that

- He is the eternal source of life and so he cannot die (Jer. 10:10; John 5:26).
- He cannot be imperfect (2 Sam. 22:31; Matt. 5:48).
- He cannot go back on his word or change his plans (Ps. 33:11; Isa. 46:10; James 1:17).
- He cannot lie (Titus 1:2; Heb. 6:18).

If God did such things he would not be God, and God cannot *not* be God. He cannot act contrary to his nature. This is not a limitation imposed on God by his creation, but an intrinsic, internal limitation. With omnipotence understood in its proper theological sense, the problem of the rock quickly vanishes.

Omnipotence simply means that God is in control of his creation and that he exercises dominion over it. That is, omnipotence does not describe God's nature so much as his relationship to the created order. If it is so understood, then the answer to the "unanswerable" question is obvious. No! God could not build a rock so big that he could not move it. To say that he could build such a rock is to say that there could be part of the creation that is outside the scope of God's control. That would deny his omnipotence. To say that God cannot build such a rock is not to deny his omnipotence, but to affirm it.

EL SHADDAI

One of the special names the Israelites used to call on God was closely connected to his almighty power. The name *El Shaddai* dates from patriarchal times. Linguistically it may come from the Hebrew verb that means "to overpower" or "to destroy." Some scholars find its origin in the words "the thunderer" or "the One who is sufficient." But the most probable meaning is "the One Who Overpowers."[2] Its frequent use in the Book of Job gives credence to this view. Job is overwhelmed by the power of God (see chapters 38–42). The might of God is revealed against all who would overthrow him. The psalmist portrays a summit meeting of the world powers who enter into a conspiracy against God:

> Why do the nations conspire and the peoples plot in vain? The kings of the earth take their stand and the rulers gather together against the LORD and against his Anointed One. "Let us break their chains," they say, "and throw off their fetters." (Ps. 2:1–3)

The response of God to these combined forces united against him is laughter. "The One enthroned in heaven laughs" (v. 4). The total might of men mustered against God is like the "mouse that roared." The foolishness of men in their war with God is matched only by their arrogance. Elsewhere the psalmist declares, "Nations are in uproar, kingdoms fall; he lifts his voice, the earth melts" (Ps. 46:6). One word from the lips of God is enough to melt the earth!

Ancient Israel looked at these images of God's might not as pictures of divine tyranny or arbitrary rule. It was Israel's great hope. The God of Israel is not impotent, but manifests himself as the King of glory:

> Lift up your heads, O you gates; be lifted up, you ancient doors, that the
> King of glory may come in.
> Who is this King of glory? The LORD strong and mighty, the LORD
> mighty in battle.
> Lift up your heads, O you gates; lift them up, you ancient doors, that
> the King of glory may come in.
> Who is he, this King of glory? The LORD Almighty—he is the King of
> glory. (Ps. 24:7–10)

RELATED RESOURCES FROM LIGONIER MINISTRIES

John Gerstner. "Handout Theology: Angels and Man," video or audio series.
———. *The Rational Biblical Theology of Jonathan Edwards.*
———. "The Theology of Jonathan Edwards," video or audio series.
R. C. Sproul. "All Christians Believe in Predestination," video.
———. "Attributes of God," audio series.
———. "Dealing with Difficult Problems," video or audio series, and outline.
———. "Themes from Ecclesiastes," video or audio series.
———. "If God Is Sovereign, How Can Man Be Free?" audio series.
———. "Introductory Logic," audio series.
———. "One Holy Passion," video or audio series. Also published in a book version, *The Character of God.*
———. "Trinity, Decrees, Creation, and Providence," video or audio series.
———. *The Holiness of God.*
———. *The Providence of God.*

**I believe in God . . . ,
Maker of heaven and earth.**

Of Chaos and Dignity

Who are you? Where are you going? The answers you give to such questions, and how you feel about yourself as you frame your responses, depend largely on how you answer another question: Where did you come from?

Toronto? Go for it, Bluejays! The Cabrini-Green projects in Chicago? You were in with your homeboys, or you were nothin', man. The Tennessee hills? They waren't much money, but we scratched by. The trash-scavenging society of Mexico City? A committed marriage? An adoption agency? A broken home with a missing dad? A one-night stand in the back seat of a Trans-Am? However you answer, emotions are attached to your thoughts, positive and negative. These feelings are building blocks of self-worth and identity.

Two more possible answers: The intentional plan and unique, personal design of a loving Creator God? A fortuitous mix of amino acids in a warm, primordial pond?

To confess that God is Creator is to confess that we are not cosmic accidents, devoid of ultimate value. We came from somewhere significant and we are headed toward a destination of importance. This is welcome news, if it is true. Twentieth-century events and philosophies have conspired to precipitate a crisis in our confidence.

Kaleidoscopic changes in every nook and cranny of life have crowded us to the brink of chaos.

- Connected to the Internet by modem I have more knowledge at my fingertips than stacked the shelves of the Library of Congress in 1900. Unfortunately, along the way to this fountain of fact I must navigate thousands of home pages hawking frivolous or offensive products and meaningless philosophies.
- My car has a more sophisticated computer than the one that guided Neil Armstrong to the moon. But the proliferation of cars and the number of places I must go multiply time spent in harm's way among irresponsible motorists.
- The technology that assembled this page of type, produced the plate, and ran the press would have transcended a nineteenth-century printer's imagining. But has technological efficiency and increased productivity given us more time to read inspiring works?
- Cell phones, satellite uplinks, and online chat groups put us in touch with the global village. But individuals seem more insulated and alone than ever before.

Restlessness bordering on despair permeates civilization at a wondrous moment in which to be alive. Unfortunately, while the new technology was being designed, old philosophies were depriving us of the joy that could have come with it. The naïve optimism of nineteenth-century humanism gave way to the skepticism of atheistic existentialism, a shadow hovering over all considerations of the meaning of existence.

. . . Maker of heaven and earth

Martin Heidegger, one of the significant voices of contemporary philosophy, sees humanity as trapped in the chaos of time.

Human beings are conscious of the passing of time, but menaced by the absence of two vital pieces of the puzzle of life. We do not know from where we have come. We do not know where, if anywhere, we are going. Thanks to gender neutrality and orientation confusion, we may not even know if we are a he or a she.

This is a state that Heidegger calls "throwness"; each person feels chaotically hurled or thrown into life, then bounced around as if caught in an earthquake. There is one certainty—death. This plight provokes angst. How a man or woman deals with this anxiety determines how "authentic" life will be. The person who succumbs to angst loses all hope of authentic existence. Authentic existence is achieved only by the courage to live freely in the face of an ominous future. Life's only meaning is brought to it by the existentialist hero. In this scenario, the creative power of humanity, not God, gives hope.

Similar strains were played by Friedrich Nietzsche, who died the year the twentieth century was born. Nietzsche formulated the foundational precepts of nihilism. God is dead, and only the nihil (nothingness) remains. There are no values or purposes, save what we create for ourselves. The inauthentic person flees into the security of the group and finds solace in the morality of the herd. Slavery to the herd is the only alternative to facing the threat of the nihil.

Existentialism did us a great service by focusing on the stark reality of chaos. Existentialists made it impossible to sweep threatening aspects of human existence under some neatly woven, metaphysical rug. They screamed "NO" to all contrived systems that fail to take seriously the human tragedy. However, existentialists leave us with no response to chaos except a blind leap of faith or equally chaotic courage. If there are no values, then existentialism has no value. Perhaps the most consistent answer to chaos in existential terms would be silence. But, of course, the existentialist feels no need to be consistent. To be consistent would be to deny life's chaos.

There are other possible responses to the human predicament. From the mechanistic determinists and hyperevolutionists come the answer that the human animal is the highest advance up a scale of life that emerged out of primordial slime. Humanity, the grown-up germ, is the result of accidental cosmic forces, and the destiny of the human race is at the mercy of these indifferent, impersonal forces. This view provides more insight into the origin of human existence. It does not leave us in total darkness about the goal of human existence, as does existentialism. That does not, however, point us in the direction of significance. What began in the slime is destined for organic disorganization or disintegration. Edward J. Carnell put it this way: "Modern man appears to be but a grown-up germ, sitting on a gear of a vast cosmic machine which is some-day destined to cease functioning because of lack of power."[1]

The mechanistic view offers no understanding of the meaning of life. Attempts have been made to develop a sense of mechanistic ethics. All have failed. Why should germs be moral? If I am a cosmic accident, why should I "give a tinker's dam" about you? Why prefer life over death? What is so special about life? Why should a human being be valued over a stone? More devastating than a hostile universe is an indifferent one.

The biblical view of creation does not retreat before the threat of chaos. In the Old Testament, the forces of chaos are closely linked with the symbol of the sea and its primordial sea monster. The ancient Israelites contrasted the threatening power of the sea with the life-giving solace of the river. Violent storms swept off the Mediterranean Sea. Attacks by seafaring Philistines were a constant source of danger. But the Jordan River gave life to the parched plain. The river's victory of life over death, of peace over violence and chaos, is seen in Psalm 46:

God is our refuge and strength,
  an ever-present help in trouble.
Therefore we will not fear, though the earth give way
  and the mountains fall into the heart of the sea,
though its waters roar and foam
  and the mountains quake with their surging.
There is a river whose streams make glad the city of God,
  the holy place where the Most High dwells.
God is within her, she will not fall;
  God will help her at break of day. (vv. 1–5)

The sea monster was a recurrent image of primordial chaos. Only in the religion of Israel is there ultimate victory over chaos. The opening of Genesis reads:

In the beginning God created the heavens and the earth. Now the earth was formless and empty, darkness was over the surface of the deep, and the Spirit of God was hovering over the waters. And God said, "Let there be light," and there was light. God saw that the light was good, and he separated the light from the darkness. (1:1–4)

The earth is formless, empty, dark as the Spirit moves over the waters, ready to act. Perhaps this indicates nothing more than the state of the as-yet-unfinished creation. Or perhaps the account is written in such a way as to highlight God's triumph over the forces of chaos. In either case, God's power extends over the void and is not left in a stand-off with chaos. God's Spirit moves—and the creative power unleashed is characterized in the consequent benediction: It was *good*.

The Christian confesses a God who has power far greater than that of chaos. The serpent seduces the man and the woman, but cannot ultimately destroy humanity. Christianity knows no eternal dualism of evil and good, yin and yang, chaos and order, Satan and Yahweh. Rather, God keeps the chaos under control. God asks Job, "Can you pull in the leviathan with a fishhook?" (Job 41:1). Here, the powerlessness of Job is set in marked contrast to the power of God. God's power over evil is so great that he casts for the primordial sea monster and catches him with a five-pound test line.

The goal of creation is never meaninglessness. The Spirit moves over the waters, and out of the abyss and the void comes order. Out of the darkness comes piercing light. The creation account moves in a rising crescendo through one day and then another until a moving climax is reached on the sixth day. On this day the crowning act of God's creation is reached: God creates humanity.

THE HUMANIST PENULTIMATE

Humanism is not a recent philosophical phenomenon. It was the ancient Greek philosopher Protagoras who issued the motto *homo mensura*, "man is the measure." In Protagoras's thinking, all virtue and ideals could be measured against the human mean. Creation ultimately exalted this ideal creature. Concern for humanity is at the heart of all forms of humanism.

Since Christianity is also deeply concerned about people, it is at some points difficult to distinguish Christianity from humanism. Both seek the healing of estranged relationships, and both honor the dignity of the human being. However, their bases for dignity are radically different. The Christian sees the horizontal, interpersonal relation as inseparable from the vertical relationship with God. To remain at the human, horizontal level is to neglect the path toward eternal human significance. The murder of Abel by Cain followed Adam and Eve's violation of God's command in the garden. The estrangement was vertical before it manifested itself horizontally. When Jesus summarized the law (Matt. 22:37–39), he appealed first to the Great Commandment of Deuteronomy 6:5, "Love the LORD your God with all your heart and with all your soul and with all your mind." On that basis he added the second commandment from Leviticus 19:18, "Love your neighbor as your-self." Humanism isolates the latter from the former, thus leaving us with a penultimate or second-best solution.

To establish human dignity without acknowledging the God of creation, the humanist must act in an arbitrary and irrational fash-ion. If humans rose by chance from chaos, why should dignity be ascribed to them? Since the advent of the Christian faith, human-ism has constantly incorporated Christian values and ethics while ripping the heart out of Christianity's theological context. Yet that context is the only reason the values and ethics make sense. As a representative human, I resent the moral demands if someone tells me I "ought" to do this or that, without giving me any reason. Hu-manists have for no reason made dignity and value the "givens" of human experience. To be sure, our experience agrees with their as-sessment. It screams that life is valuable and that each person is a creature of immense worth and dignity. That scream is hollow, however, if it comes from a germ with no destiny but death.

THE ULTIMATE

Christianity's difference lies not in the climax of the creation ac-count—the appearance of humankind on the sixth day. Rather, the climax of creation occurs on the seventh day, the day given over to rest and holiness. God rests on the Sabbath and consecrates this rest as more than a respite from labor. The Sabbath points to the end of restlessness. Where there is anxiety, there is no rest; where there is sin, there is anxiety. Where the vertical relationship be-tween humanity and God is broken, there can be no Sabbath.

The reason is that people are created to be image-bearers of God. Whatever else that involves, it certainly includes the privilege and responsibility to reflect God's glory and holiness. When we no longer show God's loveliness because of sin, then restlessness results. Where there is no holiness, chaos intrudes. People are violated. Anxiety becomes the order of the day. Sin makes us "underachievers" who are doomed, apart from Christ, to spend our days trying to compensate for our failure as true image-bearers.

In his *Confessions*, Augustine states, "O God, thou hast made us for thyself, and our hearts are restless until they find their rest in thee." Augustine gets to the heart of the matter. The murderer Cain was condemned to wander in lostness. We are all under that sentence of restlessness unless our root relationship to our Creator is restored. The Christian vision is that humanity has a reason to be, a "chief end" in the terminology of the Westminster Shorter Catechism. What is that ultimate, satisfying purpose? The Catechism answers: "Man's chief end is to glorify God and to enjoy Him forever." The connection is between glorifying God and joy. Conversely, when we dishonor God and fall short of his glory, we experience restlessness. Only obedience brings joy. The pursuit of happiness, beyond momentary pleasure, is impossible in the humanist scheme, because the humanist philosophy retreats from obedience to God.

The great human folly is to imagine that satisfaction can be found outside paradise. The wisdom of Jesus was in understanding the purpose of creation. Jesus fulfilled the image of God. As a human being, Christ had a single-hearted focus: to do the will of the Father. He commanded: "Seek first his kingdom and his righteousness, and all these things will be given to you as well" (Matt. 6:33).

HOLY GOD, FREED HUMAN

Human dignity is rooted in the holiness of God; it reflects God's dignity. People who seek to dignify themselves succumb to the primordial temptation, "You will be like God." Arrogance is not the same as dignity. Being dissatisfied with the status of being the highest of God's creatures, Adam despised his own dignity. He lusted for power and lost the dignity with which he began. Created humanity is not satisfied with freedom; people want autonomy, but find slavery instead because they cannot be God. Here Christ stands in sharp contrast to the rest of humanity. Christ was the one "who, being in very nature God, did not consider equality with God something to be grasped, but made himself nothing, taking the very nature of a servant, being made in human likeness" (Phil. 2:6–7). The first Adam was not satisfied with being in the likeness of God. He grasped arrogantly for equality with God. Jesus, a second Adam, humbly gave up equality with God for the likeness of a man. Herbert Richardson shows us the relationship of God's holiness to his dignity. He says:

> The *kabod* (glory) is not His nature, or essence; it does not define what God is. Nor is God's *kabod* His very existence, for the word *kabod* cannot be used as a proper name. Rather, God's *kabod* is the weightiness, heaviness, degree, or dignity proper to His being who He is. . . . Holiness refers neither to essence (i.e., to an attribute of God's nature) nor to existence (i.e., to God's very being); rather it is a dignity.[2]

In this schema, the holiness of God is the totality of who God is. Thus, when we speak of God's holiness or glory (or anything else), we are dealing with God's dignity. The word *dignity* is difficult to define, yet many rocks have been thrown and marches made over the issue of human dignity. We instinctively grasp something of its meaning, but clear definitions are rare. Again, Richardson is helpful:

> Dignity is the basis of authority. It is what gives weight to words, i.e., turns them into commands.
> Dignity is the basis of tragedy. It is what gives life importance and redeems it from triviality.
> Dignity is the basis of meaning. It is not identical with meaning. . . . Even though life may have meaning, it may not have dignity.[3]

Richardson connects dignity with value and worth. An example is the way we perceive crime and its victims. At one point in history, the city of Boston was a battleground for mobsters. More than thirty gangland killings took place within a short time. The citizens took notice, but there was no vociferous public demand for action until an attorney was severely maimed in an attack. At once the outcry began. The public shock over the attempted murder of a law-abiding citizen was far greater than complaints about a war among criminals.

Distinctions of human dignity are often made in public perceptions. In 1963, an entire generation was traumatized by the shooting of an American president. So great was national and international grief that namesake landmarks memorializing John F. Kennedy began popping up everywhere. New York's Idlewild International Airport became Kennedy International Airport. The portion of Cape Canaveral on which the space center was located became Cape Kennedy. Schools, highways, and buildings all over the world were renamed to commemorate Kennedy. Yet this was a double homicide. A police officer also was killed, probably by the same assassin. Why don't we have a Tippet International Airport? The answer is that Kennedy's person was all tied up with his office as president of the United States. He had extraordinary dignity by virtue of his office.

The political realities of the entire Middle East region were shaken by the November 1995 shooting of Israel's prime minister Yitzhak Rabin. His was one of hundreds of lives lost to violent attacks in the Middle East during the 1990s—but his was the one that had the most enduring consequences. The main reason was the official dignity of his office.

Distinctions of dignity are built into our very vocabulary. In English we reserve titles of distinction for academic attainments. Judges and elected officials are accorded special note. John Smith sounds a whole lot more important when he is called "Dr. Smith," "the honorable Congressman Smith," or "President Smith."

But "Germ Smith" just doesn't have the same ring. People do not build monuments to germs. Few people grieve when a fly dies.

This is not just a semantic or historical matter. The value difference between humanist and creation visions of human worth has profound significance. Martin Luther King Jr. did not give his life to advance the cause of equal civil rights for black germs. Many thousands now work tirelessly in the right to life movement, but not to save the lives of preborn viruses. Although at the gut level we automatically assume the dignity of human beings, it is pure nonsense apart from creation.

Creation has always been at the center of the value war over the intrinsic worth of a person. But it no longer is the sole center. When Jesus Christ laid aside deity and took on a human nature, that act alone forever elevated human worth. In Christ the goal of creation is realized. He is the standard of human dignity. No wonder we cannot go a city block in any major city of the Western world without finding some symbol relating to Christ. His cross is everywhere. Every second a clock ticks a group of people somewhere is gathered at a table eating a meal "in remembrance of" him. The world hungers for the dignity of Christ.

THE "HOW" OF CREATION

One of the most stormy issues of the twentieth century related to the Maker of heaven and earth has been the "how" of creation. Various scientific theories have been postulated. None can be finally demonstrated, as they involve events of an early history that no one today can observe or test. There are three philosophical alternatives in this debate: (1) the world is self-created; (2) the world is eternally self-existent; or (3) the world was created by something or someone outside itself who is self-existent.

The first alternative is a logical absurdity. For the world to be self-created presupposes that the world exists so that it can create itself. For something to create itself, it has to be there before it is there. The second alternative raises serious scientific questions. To posit that the universe is self-existent is to posit that the universe is eternal. Some theories take such a position, but with enormous scientific consequences. The third alternative is that the universe was created by something or someone who is eternal and has the power of existence in himself. One thing is absolutely certain. If *anything* exists now, then *something* has always existed. Something or someone is eternal. To dispute this is to retreat to the absurdity of the first alternative. The issue is not whether something is eternal; *something* is. The question is *what* is eternal.

Biblical faith does not give a scientific description of the origin of the universe, but it does give an answer to the *Who* of creation. The how is given in theological terms. God calls the world into existence *ex nihilo* (out of nothing). The Bible describes creation in terms of the awesome power of God's commands by divine imperative or fiat. God orders the world to be, and it is. The power of God's authority is graphically displayed when Christ calls Lazarus from the dead in John 11. When Jesus comes to the tomb, Lazarus has already been dead four days. The succinct report of Lazarus's condition was that "by this time there [was] a bad odor" (v. 39). Jesus did not enter the tomb and administer mouth-to-mouth resuscitation. He ordered Lazarus back to life. We are told, "Jesus called in a loud voice, 'Lazarus, come out!'" (v. 43b). The dead man arose.

Paul says that God "gives life to the dead and calls things that are not as though they were" (Rom. 4:17). In biblical language, God manifests his authority over all creation. This is not a belief in spontaneous generation, but in spontaneous creation. The Scriptures aren't interested in vain speculation about these things. Augustine's reply to the Greeks who asked, "What was God doing before he created the world?" was that "he was creating hell for curious souls!" Our confession of faith in God's act of creation is not a flight into the absurd, but an expression of confidence founded in God's self-revelation. For good reason we affirm that life is meaningful and that human dignity is not some empty fantasy.

CREATOR TO CREATION

The question of God's relationship to his creation has been a difficult and controversial issue throughout the history of the Christian church. The pendulum has swung between the polar extremes of radical *transcendence* (deism) and radical *immanence* (pantheism). The transcendence of God refers to his place above and apart from creation. Transcendence seeks a clear differentiation between the Creator and his creation. Radical transcendence views God as being totally isolated from the world. He exists, but his existence never touches human history—save at the point of creation. God created the world, but he never stoops to involve himself in it. He is First Cause or Prime Mover, but is now, at best, a disinterested spectator. One of the simplest varieties of radical transcendence can be seen in eighteenth-century deism. The deists viewed the world as a closed mechanical system that operated solely on the basis of fixed internal natural laws. God was the heavenly Watchmaker who made the intricate parts of the clock, wound it up, and then left it alone to operate as any other machine. God's only involvement was in the making, assembling, and ordering of the parts according to his own design. In this, God "rules" or "governs" the machine by the internal laws at work within the machine itself.

Although deism developed historically as a conscious alternative to the Christian faith, the "synthesis-seekers" of the eighteenth century sought to adapt deist naturalism to classical Christian teachings. They came up with several varieties of naturalistic Christianity. All recorded intrusions into history by God were interpreted out of the biblical narratives. Supernatural events and miracles were relegated to the level of primitive mythology. They cannot be taken seriously as historical events, but they still have didactic value in an ethical or existential sense. Others simply explained them away in purely natural terms. For example, Jesus did not really feed five thousand people with a few loaves and fish. That would require divine power at work in the human sphere. This was instead an "ethical miracle." Jesus prevailed on people who had enough foresight to bring hefty lunches to the occasion and thus could share their abundance with those who had brought nothing to eat. Thus, Jesus' ethical influence performed a miracle of "sharing" that overcame normal human selfishness.

An interesting entertainment news item illustrates the continuing influence of this view. A popular entertainer who bore a child out of wedlock and has stood as an antithesis to morality has stated that she plans to read the Bible to her child. She will, of course, be sure that her child understands that these are all just stories, but they do teach us important lessons about how to live.

The radically transcendent God inspires the telling of stories but he would never be able to hear the groans of his people and act to liberate them from bondage in Egypt. There is no room for talk of a personal relationship to a covenant Lord who commits himself to a nation or to an individual. Prayer becomes a therapeutic soliloquy. Incarnation becomes a Gnostic redeemer myth. Radical transcendence removes God so far from history that, practically speaking, there is little difference between God and no God. God is dead; at least his relationship to the world is dead and gone, and we are left with an impersonal machine as the object of our devotion.

At the other extreme are the radical immanentists, who closely identify God with the totality of things. The simplest form is pantheism. Pantheism combines the words *pan* ("all") and *theos* ("god"). To say that "all is god" accurately summarizes the meaning. Here is a leap from the presence of God everywhere to the idea that God is the totality of the universe. Of course, it is one thing to say that God's work is evidenced in the beauty of a flower and quite another to say that the flower *is* God or a part of God. This distinction is not clear in crass forms of pantheism.

We need to make careful philosophical distinctions at this point so as not to label as pantheist those who are not. Many serious philosophers and theologians, especially those influenced heavily by Platonism or Neo-Platonism, have sought to define God as the ground or "power" of all existence. These people are not speaking from the standpoint of pure pantheists, whose number would include adherents of Eastern religions, astrology fanciers, wiccans, and followers of most New Age gurus. The responsibility for the confusion, though, lies partly with the thinkers' failure to adequately distinguish their views from pantheism.

Against the God who meaningfully communicates truths about creation, the dominant god of modern theologies is so immanent as to be indistinguishable from creation. One contemporary voice is process theology. Advocates, including Alfred North Whitehead, Charles Hartshorne, John Cobb, and Schubert Ogden, disagree at many points, but they unanimously reject the God of classic Christianity for a god who is continually changing. God is said to have two poles. The potential pole is infinite; the actual pole is finite. Thus, God is potentially infinite but actually finite. The potential pole is beyond this world, while the actual pole is in the physical world. As a soul relates to the body, so God inhabits the world, for the world is God's body. The world depends on God for direction, and God depends on the world for growth in perfection. Human beings, by their own efforts, can contribute to God's growth in perfection. Because God is finite, it will actually never be possible to overcome all evil. Process theology reduces God to a director who participates in the world process rather than recognizing the sovereign Creator.

The biblical view of God forbids us to define him in totally transcendent or totally immanent terms. Creation is the theater in which we view God's past and present handiwork. God must be distinguished from the world or we fall into idolatry—the worship of things rather than God. Paul severely indicts pantheism in the opening section of his Epistle to the Romans:

> Although they claimed to be wise, they became fools and exchanged the glory of the immortal God for images made to look like mortal man and birds and animals and reptiles. . . . They exchanged the truth of God for a lie, and worshiped and served created things rather than the Creator—who is forever praised. (1:22–23, 25)

God is *not* the world. He stands apart from it in authority, in power, in dignity, and in being. However transcendent God may be, he is passionately involved with his creation. His activity extends far beyond the limits of creative origins. Though not to be identified or confused with the world, he is nevertheless near to all of us:

> He will not let your foot slip—
>   he who watches over you will not slumber;
> indeed, he who watches over Israel will neither slumber nor sleep.
> The LORD watches over you—
>   the LORD is your shade at your right hand. (Ps. 122:3–5)

He is the God in whom "we live and move and have our being" (Acts 17:28). He is the God who notices the fall of the sparrow and counts the very hairs on our heads (Matt. 10:29–30). The presence of God is at the heart of the Judeo-Christian faith. It is our joy that Jesus is *Emmanuel,* "God-with-us." The Latin phrase *Deus pro nobis* ("God for us") is integral to our confession. The psalmist cries:

God is our refuge and strength,
>   an ever-present help in trouble.
Therefore we will not fear, though the earth give way
>   and the mountains fall into the heart of the sea. . . .
There is a river whose streams make glad the city of God,
>   the holy place where the Most High dwells.
God is within her, she will not fall;
>   God will help her at break of day.
Nations are in uproar, kingdoms fall;
>   he lifts his voice, the earth melts.
The LORD Almighty is with us;
>   the God of Jacob is our fortress. (Ps. 46:1–2, 4–7)

The presence of God formed the basis of Israel's faith. The mission of New Testament Israel is activity *with* Christ—action carried out in the context of the promise, "Surely I am with you always, to the very end of the age" (Matt. 28:20b). God commits himself to the world he fashioned. Thus the Apostles' Creed does not end with a statement of God's making the world, but moves quickly to God's ultimate presence, the incarnation, and to God's ultimate activity, redemption.

RELATED RESOURCES FROM LIGONIER MINISTRIES

John Gerstner. "Handout Theology: Man the Sinner; The Ten Commandments," video or audio series.

R. C. Sproul. "A Blueprint for Thinking," video or audio series, and study guide.

———. "Battle for Our Minds," video or audio series, and study guide.

———. "Christian Worldview," audio series or book.

———. "Doctrine of Sin," audio series.

———. "Modern Atheism," audio series.

———. *Not a Chance.*

———. "Nothing Left to Chance," video.

———. *Reason to Believe.*

———. "The City of Man," audio series.

———. "The History of Philosophy," audio series.

———. "The Nature of Persons," audio series.

———. "Themes from Deuteronomy," video or audio series.

———. "Themes from Genesis," video or audio series.

———. "Understanding Ethics," audio series.

I believe . . .
in Jesus Christ,
his only Son, our Lord.

The Man Who Is the Issue

To call a Christian a "theist" is roughly equivalent to calling the space shuttle *Atlantis* a "glider." Yes, it glides unpowered back through the atmosphere to a runway. But its meaning and functionality are so much more complex that "glider" is not a really helpful or accurate description. Christian faith is not *theism* in general. Christianity is *thoroughly trinitarian theism.* The God of Abraham is the God who was in Christ. Jesus Christ is not one prophet among many; he is God incarnate. Jesus is not the *exclusive* revelation of God. God is revealed in nature, in history, and, particularly, in the law, the prophets, and the apostles. But Christ is the *conclusive* revelation of God.

For clarity, we should say, "Jesus, the Christ." The words *Jesus Christ* combine a proper name and a title. *Jesus* identifies an individual who lived in first-century Palestine. He was known as Jesus of Nazareth, referring to his childhood hometown, or *Jesus bar Joseph,* relating to his parentage. He was the eldest son of Joseph and Mary. But in the role of *Christ,* Jesus became the focal point of all human history. Given the extrabiblical evidence and the profound, ongoing influence of this personage, there really isn't much room to doubt that the man Jesus of Nazareth existed. What we must learn, however, is whether Jesus was truly *the Christ*. If he was, then there are staggering implications.

Christ is a title filled with theological significance. The word is from the Greek word *christos*, which means "anointed one." It is the Greek term that translated the Old Testament Hebrew word *Messiah*. Thus, in the combined name *Jesus Christ*, a confession of faith is immediately articulated. The words mean "Jesus, the Messiah."

... and in Jesus Christ, his only Son, our Lord, ...

THE JESUS OF HISTORY

New Testament scholars have been deeply embroiled in the quest for the Jesus of history, in both the original "quest" of the nineteenth century and the "new quest" of the twentieth century. These scholars want to dig past the New Testament understanding of Jesus to get to know the "real" person. The New Testament documents do not give us an unbiased biography, but Jesus in the context of religious conviction. The Gospels are not newspaper reports. They are unabashedly biased, openly admitting their aim to persuade and convert. John writes, "These [things] are written that you may believe" (John 20:31). Details of Jesus' life are organized around a theological message and frequently interrupted by theological interpretation. Thus, the biblical record is not normal historical reportage. It is a *redemptive history*. So scholars want to fill in the details, to get behind the redemptive interpretation to the man. They desire a more objective account of who Jesus was and what he did.

The frustration of the nineteenth-century "quest" was that the Jesus(es) who emerged from the "demythologizing" investigations always seemed to be cloaked in the school of thought that was doing the investigating. The Hegelian School discovered an "idealistic" Jesus. The School of Ritschl found an "ethical teacher." The twentieth-century quest has learned enough from past mistakes to give more serious attention to the New Testament documents than did the old quest. But the results have been similar, producing an "existentialist" Jesus. Obviously the journey past the confines of the biblical record is down a speculative road. Not all speculation is invalid, nor have all the insights about Christ gathered on these quests been useless. But we do not have unlimited license to reconstruct the life of Jesus around a pet theory. In the end, we invariably must demythologize our own portraits. Otherwise imaginations run wild.

Any genuine attempt to understand Jesus of Nazareth begins with an admission that our own minds undermine our efforts. Some members of the baby buster generation did their best to sanitize their lives and surroundings of religion; now, some of their children are reaching adulthood with something approaching a tabula rasa about Jesus. But they have at least soaked up some media references and parental prejudices, which they will have to evaluate as best they can. Few Western adults approach the question of Jesus with dispassionate objectivity. Post-Christian society has been subtly immersed in varieties of Christianity—and in the rejection of Christ. A recurring cover story of secular news magazines in the mid-1990s has been the "Jesus Seminar" and other pop theology searches for relevant faith.

Too much is at stake when we confront the New Testament claims to be coldly objective about them. Whether Jesus rose from the dead is a significant question. Whether he is now King of the universe to whom every person owes allegiance is not a matter of indifference. A living Jesus with an absolute claim on my life is something I dare not ignore.

THE MYTH-MAKERS

The impossibility of total objectivity does not mean we have to abandon our pursuit of the truth about Jesus. Rather, we need to check our assumptions and conclusions for cultic subjectivism. We need to take a conservative approach to the matter, using sound scientific investigation. The study of history demands creative thinking, but not all creative thinking is valid. A genuinely creative historian can perceive and demonstrate, via proof, the motivating forces that shape events. Scholarly creativity must not be confused with fanciful imagination.

One problem is that great scholars have been able to achieve distinction only by coming up with new ideas that are politically acceptable to their colleagues. Defense of the historic Christian faith in academia today is both condemned as heretical to the cultic assumptions of modern theology and dismissed as irrelevant. One well-respected professor at a theological school changed his mind and took a stand against the atheism of his colleagues. A scandal erupted. He refused to resign. He was on tenure and thus could not be fired. He was consequently stripped of his classes and assigned to a new office—in a janitor's closet.[1] The pressures on theologians are subtle but real. The surest way to advance a career is to come up with new ideas, however wild and unbridled, rather than seek truth.

In the mid-1990s much of the attention on the historical Jesus focused on the Westar Institute and its famous "Jesus Seminar." Nothing really new about Jesus was said through the publications and media hype coming from this ongoing movement. The seminar brought together recent theories about the lost Q source that is theorized to lie behind the Synoptic Gospels (Matthew, Mark, Luke), plus some philosophical, feminist, and liberationist revisions of what Jesus taught. The difference was that these views had been presented in forms too technical for popular consumption. Liberal theologians decided that if their views were to truly revolutionize the church, they needed better media relations and effective translation of their ideas. They have accomplished this goal. Within weeks of one another, *Time* and *Newsweek* ran major cover stories lauding the new opportunity for relevant faith coming from this school of thought. The historical Jesus had become big news.

Two of the most successful Jesus Seminar theologians are Burton Mack, author of *The Lost Gospel: The Book of Q,* and John Dominic Crossan, author of *Jesus: A Revolutionary Biography.* The "historical Jesus" of Mack was a traveling Greek philosopher of the Cynic tradition and a hedonist, a sort of 1960-ish beatnik with very little interest in religion. Crossan's Jesus was more Jewish, but he had imbibed strongly of Greek philosophy. He was a peasant and social revolutionary. His own disciples attached no special significance to his death. The fiction of an atoning death and resurrection developed as the author of the Gospel of Mark used Jesus to promote his own social agenda.

If all this sounds vaguely familiar, a similar effort appeared a generation ago in a book that received considerable publicity. *The Myth of God Incarnate* was a discussion by seven scholars about whether the Christian idea of incarnation—that Jesus was God become flesh—had any viable place in modern culture. (These theologians believed it did not.) In one essay, Michael Goulder argued that the incarnation was an idea adopted from the Samaritans. Frances Young honestly admitted that she could find no similar concept in pre-Christian religion. Even its authors admitted they had nothing new to report. They were popularizing recurring themes in contemporary theology.

The most remarkable aspect of these books and essays is that they are based on no solid evidence. One theory feeds successive histories. Scholars quote one another as established fact, not noticing that each author has been building on a foundation of air. The evidence points to early publication of the Gospels, within the lifetime of those who knew Jesus. Their stories can be reconciled with one another and with what we know of the time. We have every reason to take the New Testament portrait seriously, as *redemptive* history and also as redemptive *history.* To tell a story one believes in order to convince or persuade others of its truth does not disqualify the narrator as a credible witness. Biased observers can report accurately. Whatever else we are dealing with in the Gospels, they come to us from men who claim to be eyewitnesses. Luke says:

> Many have undertaken to draw up an account of the things that have been fulfilled among us, just as they were handed down to us by those who from the first were eyewitnesses and servants of the word. Therefore, since I myself have carefully investigated everything from the beginning, it seemed good also to me to write an orderly account for you, most excellent Theophilus, so that you may know the certainty of the things you have been taught. (Luke 1:1–4)

Peter adds:

> We did not follow cleverly invented stories when we told you about the power and coming of our Lord Jesus Christ, but we were eyewitnesses of his majesty. (2 Peter 1:16)

Paul replied to a Roman official who questioned his sanity:

> "I am not insane, most excellent Festus," Paul replied. "What I am saying is true and reasonable. The king is familiar with these things, and I can speak freely to him. I am convinced that none of this has escaped his notice, because it was not done in a corner." (Acts 26:25–26)

No courtroom declaration could be more adamant than John's:

> That which was from the beginning, which we have heard, which we have seen with our eyes, which we have looked at and our hands have touched— this we proclaim concerning the Word of life. The life appeared; we have seen it and testify to it, and we proclaim to you the eternal life, which was with the Father and has appeared to us. We proclaim to you what we have seen and heard, so that you also may have fellowship with us. And our fellowship is with the Father and with his Son, Jesus Christ. (1 John 1:1–3)

People do claim to be eyewitnesses to events they never saw. And even genuine eyewitnesses can be mistaken. Eyewitnesses have been discredited because they embellished the facts with fantasy. Festus thought Paul's testimony was utter madness. However unreliable eyewitness testimony may be, we should assume, unless given reasons to believe the contrary, that it is of more value than speculative hearsay. One who cannot accept that the New Testament documents are inspired of God must at least grant that these documents must be normative for our understanding of the Jesus of history. These documents are the primary sources for our knowledge of Jesus. To dismiss their reliability by canons of speculative hypothesis is not an affront to piety so much as an affront to science. No judicious quest for historical knowledge begins with a predetermined view of what could or could not have happened. To make the facts *fit* rather than *determine* the theory is strange science.

JESUS—MESSIAH

The New Testament bears witness to the fact that the contemporaries of Jesus reacted to him with astonishment. But what is astonishing can still be credible. Voluminous research into the basic historical integrity of the New Testament documents shows impressive accuracy. The Gospel of Luke, for example, is so accurate that Luke has been called the most trustworthy historian of antiquity.[2]

Rudolf Bultmann conceded that one thing is surely true historically: The early church had a profound faith in the Jesus of history. *Is the picture of Jesus found in the New Testament a result of the creative faith of the early church, or is the faith of the early church a result of the accurate picture of Jesus found in the New Testament?*

The title *Messiah* has, from the beginning, conjured up hopes and notions. In first-century Palestine, several varieties of messianic expectancy collided. Different strands of messianic hope can already be found in the Old Testament. Jesus was constantly plagued by popular misconceptions of his messianic role, due in part to the multi-faceted Old Testament picture of the coming "Anointed One." But three main strands of messianic expectancy culminated in the work of Jesus. Christ was preeminently (1) the *Davidic king*, a royal messiah; (2) the *Son of Man*, an apocalyptic heavenly being; and (3) the *Suffering Servant* of Isaiah, a redeeming sacrifice.

Son of David

The most popular and expected Messiah-type was the Davidic king. The Old Testament reign of David was Israel's day of blessing. David excelled as a military hero and a monarch. His military exploits extended the frontiers of the nation from Dan to Beersheba. During David's rule, Israel emerged as a regional power of great strength and prosperity. The golden age was tarnished under Solomon's building program, and it turned to rust when the nation split under Jeroboam and Rehoboam. But the memory of exaltation lived on even under the oppression of Rome. The people looked to God for the Son of David who would restore the glory of Israel.

The frenzy of expectation surrounding hope of a political Messiah was not born simply in nostalgia. Old Testament prophecies gave substance to such hope. In the Psalms, David is seen as a king anointed by Yahweh. Psalm 78 declares: "From tending the sheep [Yahweh] brought [David] to be the shepherd of his people Jacob, of Israel his inheritance" (v. 71). Yahweh also promised David future exaltation:

> The LORD swore an oath to David,
> > a sure oath that he will not revoke:
> "One of your own descendants I will place on your throne." (Ps. 132:11)

> I will establish his line forever,
> > his throne as long as the heavens endure. . . .
> I will not take my love from him,
> > nor will I ever betray my faithfulness.

I will not violate my covenant or alter what my lips have uttered.
Once for all, I have sworn by my holiness—and I will not lie to
   David—
    that his line will continue forever
    and his throne endure before me like the sun;
   it will be established forever like the moon,
    the faithful witness in the sky. (Ps. 89:29, 33–36)

Throughout Israel's history, the hope of the restoration of David's throne was revived again and again in times of crisis. God promised through the prophet Amos: "In that day I will restore David's fallen tent. I will repair its broken places, restore its ruins, and build it as it used to be" (9:11). The fact that Jesus was of the line of Judah, to whom the "scepter" was promised in Genesis 49:10, and that he was born in the city of David and was David's descendant, was not regarded as coincidence by the New Testament writers. They saw the hope of a royal Messiah fulfilled in the person of Jesus. This is clearly seen in the central importance given to the ascension of Jesus. He is the Son of David, who entered heaven to inaugurate the kingdom of God.

Jesus' role as king is often confused by the frequent conflicts between Jesus and those who had misconceptions of what his kingship involved. He repudiated efforts of the people to crown him. He replied to Pilate, "My kingdom is not of this world" (John 18:36). But that does not mean that Jesus repudiated the idea of Davidic kingship. His teaching had to do with the coming of the kingdom of God. He instructed his disciples to pray for the coming of the kingdom. His vision of the kingdom was not one of a futuristic expectation. It had already begun, though it was not yet totally realized. Jesus' reign was "already," but "not yet."

It is interesting that the final question the disciples asked their Teacher before he left this earth had to do with the kingdom: "Lord, are you at this time going to restore the kingdom to Israel?" (Acts

1:6). The political restoration was still a burning issue. One might have expected Jesus to reply with some frustration: "Haven't you gotten it *yet?* How many times do I have to tell you I'm not going to restore the kingdom to Israel?" Instead, he replied: "It is not for you to know the times or dates the Father has set by his own authority" (Acts 1:7). So the question is not *whether* Jesus will restore the kingdom; the question is *when.* Jesus reigns, but his reign has not yet reached its culmination.

When we confess that Jesus is Christ we necessarily include in that confession that he is King. The significance of this confession is often lost to Westerners, who find the concept of monarchy alien and even repugnant. This rule is altogether different from the ceremonial power of the House of Windsor. Christ, as cosmic King, holds absolute sovereign authority.

Son of Man

Jesus' title *Son of Man* in the New Testament is fraught with confusion. Though the term is infrequently used by New Testament writers to refer to Jesus, they are careful to indicate the consistent use of the term by Jesus himself (eighty-one of eighty-four occurrences). From this we see that the writers were solicitous not to read their favorite titles back into the lips of Jesus, and we gain real insight into Jesus' self-understanding. "Son of Man" seems by far to have been Jesus' most frequent self-designation.[3] In contrast to *Son of God, Son of Man* would seem to refer to Jesus as a human. However, *Son of Man* more clearly implies deity than does *Son of God.* By it, Jesus clearly identified himself with the Old Testament apocalyptic Messiah in Daniel. The figure of the Son of Man is eschatological. That is, the Son of Man will manifest himself in the future, at the "end of time." He is a transcendent figure, a heavenly being who will descend to judge.

In the Book of Daniel, the Son of Man appears in a vision of heaven. He is presented before the throne of the "Ancient of Days" and "was given authority, glory and sovereign power; all peoples, nations and men of every language worshiped him. His dominion is an everlasting dominion that will not pass away, and his kingdom is one that will never be destroyed" (Dan. 7:14). The Son of Man links with the Son of David. Both are involved in kingship, dominion, and power. But the Son of David is an earthly figure whereas the Son of Man is a heavenly being.

The testimony of the New Testament to the preexistence of Jesus is inseparably related to the *Son of Man* motif. He is "from above" (John 8:23); he is "sent" from the Father. Jesus as Son of Man descended and then ascended. "No one has ever gone into heaven except the one who came from heaven—the Son of Man" (John 3:13; cf. Eph. 4:10).

It is not enough to declare that the New Testament writers confess that Jesus is a heavenly being; so is an angel. Christ is described in language reserved for deity alone. It is interesting to compare the graphic description of Daniel's Ancient of Days (Dan. 7:9–10) with John's description of the Son of Man in the Book of Revelation (Rev. 1:12–16; 5:11–12).

The Son of Man is a figure of splendor and power. He is deity, as is seen in the Old Testament portrait and in Jesus' self-understanding. Jesus links the Son of Man with creation by saying that "the Son of Man is Lord of the Sabbath" (Matt. 12:8; Mark 2:28; Luke 6:5). To claim lordship over the Sabbath is to claim lordship over creation. The Sabbath was an ordinance given by the Lord of creation. Jesus made a point of forgiving a paralyzed man of his sins "that you [the Pharisees and the teachers of the law] may know that the Son of Man has authority on earth to forgive sins" (Luke 5:24). Here was a privilege of God alone. The Jews did not miss the inference. They sought to kill Jesus because his claim to deity came through loud and clear.

We must not overstate the case and assume that the title *Son of Man* had nothing to do with Jesus' humanity and real humiliation. The scandal of Jesus' teaching about himself revolved around his suffering. He said: "The Son of Man has no place to lay his head" (Matt. 8:20); "The Son of Man is going to suffer at their hands" (Matt. 17:12); "The Son of Man did not come to be served, but to serve, and to give his life as a ransom for many" (Matt. 20:28). The heavenly being entered fully into our humanity.

Because Paul never refers to Jesus as the Son of Man, it has been argued that the apostle's concept of Christ was inconsistent with Jesus' own understanding. However, Oscar Cullmann has convincingly shown that Paul's Christology is closely related to Jesus' elaboration of the Old Testament understanding of the Son of Man.[4] The concept, if not the term, runs throughout his thinking. One of Paul's favorite descriptions of Christ is as "the second Adam." Remembering the parallel relationship between Son of Man and second Adam, Paul sets the second Adam in striking contrast to the first Adam:

> For as in Adam all die, so in Christ all will be made alive. . . . So it is written: "The first man Adam became a living being"; the last Adam, a life-giving spirit. The spiritual did not come first, but the natural, and after that the spiritual. The first man was of the dust of the earth, the second man from heaven. As was the earthly man, so are those who are of the earth; and as is the man from heaven, so also are those who are of heaven. And just as we have borne the likeness of the earthly man, so shall we bear the likeness of the man from heaven. (1 Cor. 15:22, 45–49)

Elsewhere, notably in Romans 5:12–19, Paul elaborates on the contrast. The legacy of Adam is death; the legacy of Christ is life. Adam excels in disobedience; Christ excels in obedience. Adam receives the gift of life; Christ is the giver and source of life. Adam is of the earth; Christ accepted humiliation. All that Paul says of the second Adam describes the Son of Man. The Son of Man is the mediator and champion of the new covenant. This title is our clearest biblical expression of the dual human-divine nature of Jesus.

The figure of the Son of Man lies behind the classic Western Christology of the Council of Chalcedon (A.D. 451). Christ is *vere Deus* and *vere homo*—"truly God and truly man."

Suffering Servant

Debate has raged over the years about who wrote the Book of Isaiah and the identity of the "Suffering Servant." But no one doubts that the New Testament authors found in Jesus the ultimate fulfillment of that messianic figure. That Jesus conceived his own ministry in terms of Isaiah's prophecies is clear from his sermon in the synagogue at Nazareth that marked the beginning of his public ministry. Jesus used Isaiah 61 to keynote his mission. Luke tells us:

> He found the place where it is written: "The Spirit of the Lord is on me, because he has anointed me to preach good news to the poor. He has sent me to proclaim freedom for the prisoners and recovery of sight for the blind, to release the oppressed, to proclaim the year of the Lord's favor." Then he rolled up the scroll, gave it back to the attendant and sat down. The eyes of everyone in the synagogue were fastened on him, and he began by saying to them, "Today this scripture is fulfilled in your hearing." (4:17b–21)

Jesus confirmed his declaration by both his words and his actions. He preached the good news to the poor and brought healing to the sick and liberation to the oppressed. When John the Baptist had doubts and sent messengers to ask Jesus if he were the Messiah, Jesus responded:

> Go back and report to John what you have seen and heard: The blind receive sight, the lame walk, those who have leprosy are cured, the deaf hear, the dead are raised, and the good news is preached to the poor. Blessed is the man who does not fall away on account of me. (Luke 7:22–23)

Clearly, Jesus' understanding of his mission cannot be understood simply in terms of his relationship to David or to the Son of Man. Not accidentally is Isaiah the most frequently quoted prophet in the New Testament. Jesus defined his life in terms of Isaiah 61. However, it is the relationship of his death to Isaiah's view of the Suffering Servant in Isaiah 53 that has most fully grasped the attention of the New Testament writers.

The description of Isaiah's Suffering Servant reads like an eyewitness account of the passion. No wonder Isaiah's "Servant" informed the New Testament understanding of the cross. We find ourselves standing in solidarity among the offenders for whom Christ died. We see the Father impute our sin to the atoning sacrifice. Here is the scandal of the cross and the central purpose of our Lord's suffering as a way of redemption. John calls him "the Lamb of God who takes away the sin of the world." He is the Sin-bearer.

As nowhere else in Scripture, Isaiah 53 rings with the refrain *Deus pro nobis* ("God for us"). As Karl Barth has pointed out, the servanthood of Jesus can be summarized in one Greek word, *hyper,* translated "in behalf of."[5] The one dies for the many. Any translation of the life and work of Jesus that fails to take this aspect seriously does radical violence to the New Testament text.

PROPHET, PRIEST, KING

Christ's work is described in terms of a threefold office. Christ is a *Prophet,* a *Priest,* and a *King.* As Prophet, Jesus speaks for God. He is the *Logos,* God's supreme and decisive word. The Old Testament office of prophet reaches its ultimate fulfillment in him. Like the Old Testament prophets, Jesus both foretells and forthtells. And he himself is the supreme object of Old Testament prophecies. As Priest, Jesus represents the people before God. Not only does he *offer* the supreme sacrifice, but he *is* the supreme sacrifice. He is our forever priest, the only one we require. Thus as Prophet, Priest, and King, Jesus fulfills the tripartite dimensions of the Old Testament messianic expectancy. The one who is Prophet, Priest, and King is also the Son of Man, the Suffering Servant, and the Son of David. One of the most amazing aspects of the work of Jesus is that he brings together in one person and one ministry all the many dimensions of Old Testament messianism. Cullmann says of this:

> Both the "Suffering Servant" and the "Son of Man" already existed in Judaism. But Jesus' combination of precisely these two titles was something completely new. "Son of Man" represents the highest conceivable declaration of exaltation in Judaism: "Servant of the Lord" is the expression of the deepest humiliation. Even if there really was a concept of a suffering Messiah in Judaism, it cannot be proved that suffering was combined precisely with the idea of the Son of Man coming on the clouds of heaven. This is the unheard-of new act of Jesus, that he united these two apparently contradictory tasks in his self-consciousness, and that he expressed that union in his life and teaching.[6]

Perhaps the most striking New Testament conjunction of Christ's humiliation and exaltation is the imagery of Revelation 5. John is given a vision into heaven as the all-important sealed scroll is to be opened. He hears the cry of the angel, "Who is worthy to break the seals and open the scroll?" (v. 2). No voice answers, for none are worthy of the task. John's disappointment gives way to grief.

But an elder consoles him. "Do not weep! See, the Lion of the tribe of Judah, the Root of David, has triumphed. He is able to open the scroll and its seven seals" (v. 5). Abruptly the mood of the narrative changes; a sense of expectancy replaces John's despair:

> Then I saw a Lamb, looking as if it had been slain, standing in the center of the throne, encircled by the four living creatures and the elders. . . . He came and took the scroll from the right hand of him who sat on the throne. . . . And they sang a new song:

"You are worthy to take the scroll
  and to open its seals,
because you were slain,
  and with your blood you purchased men for God
  from every tribe and language and people and nation.
You have made them to be a kingdom and priests to serve our God,
  and they will reign on the earth." (vv. 6b–9)

The drama of the Apocalypse incorporates the response of the heavenly court to the Messiah. Our confession, "We believe in Jesus, the Christ," ascribes to Jesus the highest liturgy of praise.

HIS ONLY SON, OUR LORD

The creed speaks of Jesus as the only Son of God. The title *Son of God* appeals to the claim of deity. The term, however, is a complex one with several nuances of meaning. Surely it is one of the richest titles given to Jesus in the New Testament.

Paul van Buren, one of the notorious 1960s Death of God theologians, questioned the use of this title as a confession of Christ's deity. He pointed out that in the Old Testament *Son of God* designated Israel and the king or high priest who especially represented the covenant.[7] Van Buren stated that Western Christians have used *Son* to describe the nature of Jesus, borrowing from the Greeks. In Greek categories the being of the Father is shared by the being of the Son. Therefore, if Jesus is Son, he is of the same essence as the Father.

The meaning of the title *Son of God* was at the center of the Arian controversy that culminated in the formulation of the Nicene Creed in A.D. 325. At Nicea the church confessed that Christ is "of the same substance" as the Father. That is, Jesus had a divine nature. Radical theologians have argued that the title *Son of God* has nothing to do with the function or office of Christ. It instead describes Christ's work.

There is superficial truth in this. The Bible does not reserve the term *Son of God* exclusively for Jesus. The term *Son of God* or *Sons of God* is only used in Genesis 6:2, 4, where the meaning is unclear, and Job 1:6 and 2:1, where it refers to created spiritual beings in general. God occasionally refers to Israel or Judah as "my son(s)" as a term of covenant intimacy rather than a description of covenant work (see, for example, Exod. 4:23; Jer. 10:20; Ezek. 21:10; Hos. 11:1). Isaiah 43:6–7 extends beyond national to spiritual Israel, to everyone "who is called by my name." This passage is messianic, but it does not refer to the Messiah as a Son. Passages calling David "my son" have definite messianic overtones, especially Psalm 2:7. Solomon is referred to as "my son" in 1 Chronicles 22:10 and 28:6. Several New Testament texts identify believers as adopted sons of God in Christ. The evidence is scanty that the term *Son of God* extends beyond Jesus, but we should remain cautious. The concept of sonship does extend to a wider field within the covenant.

The problem increases when we read the biblical statements of the "begottenness" of Jesus. These occur mostly in the older translations. Modern versions avoid using the term because its English meaning has changed over the centuries. They have tried to express the idea of "procession"—one thing proceeds from another. That doesn't quite catch it either. The Greek certainly doesn't teach that Jesus was ultimately "born" of the Father in the sense of a created being. John 1:14 in the King James Version calls Jesus "the only begotten of the Father." The New International Version has "the One and Only, who came from the Father," which is more correct but sounds like a fast-food version of a five-star restaurant's *chicken a la orange*.

We cannot isolate the title *Son of God* from references to the begottenness of Christ. Colossians refers to Jesus as "firstborn over all creation," and then gives a helpful interpretive reference point a few verses later, calling Jesus the "firstborn from the dead" (1:15, 18).

The author of Hebrews calls Jesus the "firstborn into the world" (1:6). These are favorite proof texts of Mormons and Jehovah's Witnesses, who argue that Jesus is a created being. The latter acknowledge that Jesus is exalted above all other creatures; indeed, Jesus even functions as the preexistent Creator. Nevertheless, Jehovah's Witnesses would never consider Christ to be God. They and many others deny the Trinity on the basis of the "sonship" of Christ.

What is at issue between Christianity and nontrinitarian sects is precisely the debate that raged in the fourth-century Arian controversy. Arius argued that one cannot be both "begotten" and "eternal." To this, the church replied that Christ was "eternally begotten," which is a stretch in both logic and semantics. This is not simply theoretical speculation. It presses on the central nerve of the life of the church—worship. It was the basis of hostility between Jesus and his contemporaries. To give worship to Christ if he is less than God is to engage in heinous idolatry. If Jesus was only a creature, he deserved his ghastly death. Jesus wasn't killed because he told people to love each other, but precisely because he claimed the prerogatives of Godhood.

We can avoid much confusion over the terms *Son of God* and *begotten* if we leave behind Greek and modern English categories of thought and return to Semitic concepts. To an ancient Hebrew, *begotten* was not descriptive of biological origin, but of a unique relationship. This is why Matthew's Gospel opens with a genealogy that traces Jesus' ancestry to David through Joseph, who was not his biological father. The parent–child unity, once formed, was every bit as strong a family identification as blood lines. When the Council of Nicea confessed that Christ was "begotten, not made," they were not retreating into irrational paradox, but were seeking to articulate the point that the Father and the Son are one. That is an eternal connection of the closest sort. The author of Hebrews presents the supremacy of the Son over the angels by referring to the Father–Son unity (1:5–6). Christ is exalted above the heavenly host with the command that he is to be worshiped. Jesus received worship from Thomas and evidently found that to be in line with the rigid monotheism of Israel. The Father is honored when the Son is worshiped because Father and the Son are one.

The Jehovah's Witnesses justify giving worship to Jesus by acknowledging that he is "a" god. When John says clearly, "The Word was God" (John 1:1), the Jehovah's Witnesses find great significance in the absence of the definite article. John does not say Jesus was *the* God, but only that he *was* "a god." This kind of exegesis doesn't take into account common Greek usage. It makes Jesus less than *the* God, but leaves us with the crassest kind of polytheism.

His "Only" Son

When the creed inserts the word *only*, the term suggests another kind of uniqueness. Other individuals in Scripture may be called sons; Christ alone is the "only begotten." He is uniquely connected to, and proceeds from, the Father. The word *only* suggests one of a kind. There is a qualitative difference between the united relationship of Christ to the Father and the godward intimacy of any other person. Here the Semitic idiom expresses the uniqueness of Christ's person and work. The Begotten One is not a creature created for a unique task, but is Very God of Very God, the second person of the Trinity. In his incarnate labor, he subordinates himself to the Father for our sake. Philippians 2 is significant:

Your attitude should be the same as that of Christ Jesus:

Who, being in very nature God,
   did not consider equality with God something to be grasped,
but made himself nothing,

taking the very nature of a servant,
being made in human likeness.
And being found in appearance as a man,
he humbled himself
and became obedient to death—
even death on a cross! (vv. 5–8)

OUR LORD

In confessing Christ as Lord, the Apostles' Creed echoes the primary confession of faith of the apostolic church. The first creed was the simple statement, "Jesus is Lord." The title *Lord* is the most exalted title given to Jesus. In the culture contemporary with the New Testament, the title *kyrios* ("lord") had various usages. It was sometimes merely a polite form of address, as in the greeting, "Dear sir." It also designated a slaveowner or master. The apostle Paul refers to himself as a "slave" (*doulos*) of the "Lord" (*Kyrios*) Jesus Christ. The slave lord purchased, owned, and governed his slaves. This connotation is used in a figurative sense frequently in the New Testament.

The title *lord* was used in a more exalted sense to refer to those of imperial power and authority. The church faced a crisis when it was required to recite the formula *Kyros Kaisar* (Caesar is Lord) in giving a loyalty oath to the emperor. The imperial title was filled with theological and religious connotations. Cullmann points out: "According to the ancient view, lordship over the world empire indicates lordship over the cosmos."[8] Hence many Christians chose to die rather than utter the loyalty oath. This refusal to call Caesar "lord" did not come out of revolutionary civil disobedience, but from reluctance to render to Caesar that which did not properly belong to him. Absolute authority, dominion, and power belonged to Christ, who alone reigns as cosmic Lord.

Some quibble that, with such a range of uses, *Lord* may not mean anything special in the New Testament references to Jesus. We could be looking at merely the courteous address of "sir." That argument will not do, however, because each occurrence has a context that usually tells quite plainly what belongs. Jesus does not call himself the "sir" of the Sabbath. Thomas does not say to Jesus, "My sir and my God." The exalted nature of the title can also be seen where the superlative form appears. When Jesus is called "Lord of lords," there is no doubt what is meant. Absolute authority over all lesser authorities is clearly indicated.

Most significant about the title *Lord* is its relationship to the Old Testament. The Greek translation of the Old Testament (the Septuagint) used the term *Kyrios* to translate the Hebrew word *Adonai*, which was a title for God himself. The Hebrew word *Yahweh*, which was the ineffable "name" of God, was too sacred to be used frivolously, even in worship. When a public reader came to *Yahweh* in the liturgy, the substitute word pronounced in its place was *Adonai*. *Adonai* was the title that indicated God's absolute authority and power.[9]

In some English translations of the Old Testament, both *Yahweh* and *Adonai* are translated "Lord." To indicate which Hebrew word is referred to, a formal distinction in printing is used. When Yahweh is to be translated, the word is in small capital letters, "LORD." When *Adonai* is behind the text, it is "Lord," printed in upper- and lowercase letters: For example, Psalm 8 begins in the New International Version, "O LORD, our Lord, how majestic is your name in all the earth!" A strict rendering from the Hebrew would be, "O *Yahweh*, our *Adonai*, how excellent. . . ." *Yahweh* is the "name" of God; *Adonai* is the "title" of God. This would be compared somewhat with the expression, President Woodrow Wilson. "Woodrow" was Wilson's name; "President" was his title, which indicated his role or function. Psalm 110 reads, "The LORD says to my Lord: Sit at my right hand. . . ." Here *Yahweh* speaks to *Adonai,* who is David's Lord and seats him at his right hand. In the New Testament, Jesus is the One who is elevated to the right hand of God and receives the title *Kyrios.* This is the name that is "above every name, . . . that at the name of Jesus every knee should bow, in heaven and on earth and under the earth, and every tongue confess that Jesus Christ is Lord, to the glory of God the Father" (Phil. 2:9b, 11).

That Jesus is objectively *the* Lord is a common assertion of the New Testament. He is the imperial authority of the entire creation. His authority has cosmic proportions. But the creed confesses not only that he is *the* Lord, but that he is *our* Lord. At the heart of the Christian faith is the believer's personal submission to the authority of God's exalted King. The confession is, in itself, meaningless. Jesus said, "Many will say to me on that day, 'Lord, Lord, did we not prophesy in your name, and in your name drive out demons and perform many miracles?' Then I will tell them plainly, 'I never knew you. Away from me, you evildoers!'" (Matt. 7:22–23). To say "Lord" and mean all that it implies cannot be done apart from the Holy Spirit.

RELATED RESOURCES FROM LIGONIER MINISTRIES

John Gerstner. "Handout Theology: Jesus Christ the Savior," video or audio series.

Art Lindsley and R. C. Sproul. "Basic Theology," audio series.

R. C. Sproul. "Face to Face with Jesus," video or audio series, and outline.

———. "Luke Interact," audio series and study notebook.

———. "The Doctrine of Christ," audio series.

———. "The Majesty of Christ," video or audio series, and study guide.

———. "Ultimate Issues," video or audio series, or book.

———. "Hebrews Interact," audio series and study notebook.

I believe . . .
in Jesus Christ, . . .
who was conceived by the Holy Ghost,
born of the virgin Mary.

The Virgin Had a *WHAT?*

The woman on the radio talk show line was adamant: All women must take control of their bodies. It is wrong to bring children into such a messed-up world. It only makes matters worse since there are already too many people. The radio host agreed to some of her points, but observed that if her view would become generally accepted or mandated by society, there could eventually be a shortage of inhabitants on earth.

No problem, responded the woman. We can always have more babies in test tubes.

She aced women's studies, but had a few problems in biology class.

The Apostles' Creed shifts from a general confession of faith in Christ to a few points of his life and work that are of utmost importance to our salvation. Assertions regarding the circumstances of his birth have been the most controversial. What engendered little debate in the early centuries of the church's history has become a roiling pot of polemics in the past two centuries. All the miracle narratives of the New Testament have been demythologized into oblivion by the ever-helpful higher critics, but these guardians of the historical Jesus have made his birth a point of special concern.

The virgin had a baby.

And I did just fine in biology.

. . . Who was conceived by the Holy Ghost,
Born of the Virgin Mary . . .

The virgin birth has been rejected by both naturalists and supernaturalists on a variety of grounds, ranging from the crass to the technical. Some of the more famous arguments against the virgin birth include the following.

ARGUMENT FROM SCIENCE

The most frequent objection to the virgin birth is that it is biologically impossible. In terms of fixed biological laws, it is impossible for a woman to conceive a child without being inseminated, either via sexual intercourse or artificial insemination. To have a "virgin" birth would necessitate a kind of spontaneous generation of male sperm that is totally antithetical to the laws of biology. No similar event has been duplicated in scientific experimentation.

This objection, of course, rests on the presupposition that we exist in a naturalistic, closed, mechanical universe that absolutely operates according to fixed laws. In chapter 5 we mentioned that the deists of the eighteenth century posited such a universe. Deism had a profound influence on naturalistic science, with or without the Divine Watchmaker. Were this such a universe, biological difficulty would not have been the only reason to doubt the birth of Christ. No personal God would be there to intrude into a fallen world with a plan for redeeming history and people.

But a naturalistic presupposition cannot be tested any more than can a supernaturalistic one. It is theoretical at best and at odds not only with biblical theology, but also with its own contemporary phi-losophy and methodology. The scientific method deals with theories, maxims, and laws that rest on inductive reasoning—analysis and test-ing. Since David Hume's treatment on causality in the mid–1700s, a judicious scientist speaks not of possibility and impossibility but of probability quotients. If we investigate the phenomena of conception and birth inductively and discover that, in the bodies of 10 zillion human females, conception has been caused by some form of insem-ination, in which a male sperm cell from outside the body fertilizes a female ovum, we have a strong case for a biological "law." This law is based on a probability quotient of astronomical odds. However, until every force and every reality in the universe is exhaustively examined and known, no inductive principle can become an absolute law.

That something cannot be duplicated in a controlled laboratory experiment does not mean that it never happened. No laboratory experiment can eliminate all possible variables. The variable of time is always a problem. In dealing with the virgin birth there is the possibility of a divine omnipotence variable. Try building *that* into your model. The scientist is at liberty to make a judgment about the probability of the virgin birth, but not its possibility. Perhaps this excursion into fine distinctions smacks of scholastic hair-split-ting, but this point of distinction is a crucial one. It deals with the issue of a "unique event," which is, in the final analysis, a histori-cal question, not a scientific one. The scientist explores what is hap-pening, not what has happened. On the basis of an analysis of the present, all that can be gained in terms of knowledge of the past or future is a projected probability quotient. *That the virgin birth is impossible is not a valid judgment; that, scientifically speaking, it is highly improbable is a valid judgment.*

A common critique of the Christian faith attacks at the point of miracles that involve *unique* events. The principle used to judge unique miracle reports is questionable: Since a "unique" event cannot be du-plicated or repeated, runs counter to normal experience, and cannot be verified empirically, it must be dismissed as irrelevant testimony. If this principle of epistemology were to be consistently applied to the scientific enterprise, our whole system of knowledge would fall like Chicken Little's sky. For there to be knowledge of one hundred cats, there must be knowledge of at least one cat. In the analysis of a series of facts, the first, unanalyzable fact must be accepted, or you have an infinite series of unacceptable unique events. On the basis of this critical principle, individuation of any kind would be disallowed and the taxonomy on which all science is based would disintegrate.

If the New Testament presented the virgin birth as a commonplace event, there would be reasonable grounds to seriously doubt the integrity of its human writers. However, the narration deals with an event that claims to be nothing less than unique. The principal characters have a difficult time believing what is happening. "Unique" events fill the life of Christ. Obviously the gospel of Christ is astonishing. Whether it is impossible must be judged against the wider question of the whole meaning and destiny of the universe, a system far more complicated than the normal processes of human reproduction. To disavow an event because it is unique is unscientific.

It is not strange that naturalistic science, with its closed system, disavows the possibility of the virgin birth. What is strange is why Christians have joined unbelievers in isolating the virgin birth from other miracles of Jesus. The virgin birth is certainly consistent with the total New Testament portrait of Jesus. Given our understanding of the problems Jesus came to address, such a birth was absolutely necessary to his success. So why do people affirm the resurrection of Christ and his sinlessness, yet deny the possibility that he was born in an unique way? What is more unique than a sinless man? The Christian faith stands or falls with the uniqueness of Christ. If I denied the beginning of the universe because it was unique, I could give no reason why I now exist to engage in a discussion about unique events. To say the virgin birth is possible is not to prove its truth, but at least it prevents prima facie rejection on alleged grounds that it is impossible.

ARGUMENT FROM EXEGESIS

Some, especially in the traditional liberal school of theology, argue that the New Testament does not even *teach* a virgin birth. The central point at issue is Matthew's use of Isaiah's prophecy: "The virgin will be with child and will give birth to a son, and they will call him 'Immanuel'—which means, 'God with us'" (Matt. 1:23). But Isaiah 7 says that an *alma* will bear a child. The word *alma* is not the technical term for a virgin in Hebrew. Rather, the term *bethula* is the more precise clinical word for virginity. The term *alma* more generally describes a "young woman." Hence the argument is that Isaiah and the New Testament writers never intended to teach more than that a young woman would have a baby. Isaiah's wife did just that.

This argument is invalid not only etymologically, but also contextually. The word *alma*, though not as precise as *bethula,* is not so ambiguous as the definition "young woman" might imply. It strongly suggests virginity. The same situation occurs in English usage of the three terms *virgin, young woman,* and *maiden. Virgin* denotes sexual purity in the sense of historically never having engaged in sexual intercourse. In modern terms, a "young woman" may or may not be sexually pure. *Young woman* simply provides a description of gender and age. The term *maiden* is an archaic word, used only infrequently in contemporary nomenclature. We usually find it only in poetry and old musical lyrics. *Alma* corresponds quite precisely with *maiden.* It strongly connotes virginal purity. It is not as explicit as *virgin,* but far more suggestive of sexual purity than *young woman.* Similarly, *alma* is less precise than *virgin,* but more explicit than *young woman.*

But more important than the definitions of the words is the context in which they are found. Isaiah 7 shows that the prophecy was partially fulfilled when an *alma,* Isaiah's bride, conceived in the conventional way and eventually gave birth. But this was a foreshadowing or type of the main event—the birth of Christ. Matthew and Luke are concerned that their readers understand this fact. In Luke's account of the annunciation, Mary is told by the angel Gabriel that she will conceive and bear a son. Mary replies in bewilderment, "How will this be, since I am a virgin?" (Luke 1:34). The angel responds, "The Holy Spirit will come upon you, and the power of the Most High will overshadow you. So the holy one to be born will be called the Son of God" (v. 35). The context here leaves no room for doubt as to what is being said to Mary. Of Mary's conception and the pregnancy of her cousin Elizabeth, the angel says, "For nothing will be impossible with God" (v. 37). The question of impossibility is raised precisely because what has been announced violates the canons of probability.

Matthew's account is even clearer on this point:

> This is how the birth of Jesus Christ came about: His mother Mary was pledged to be married to Joseph, but before they came together, she was found to be with child through the Holy Spirit. Because Joseph her husband was a righteous man and did not want to expose her to public disgrace, he had in mind to divorce her quietly.
>
> But after he had considered this, an angel of the Lord appeared to him in a dream and said, "Joseph son of David, do not be afraid to take Mary home as your wife, because what is conceived in her is from the Holy Spirit." . . .
>
> When Joseph woke up, he did what the angel of the Lord had commanded him and took Mary home as his wife. But he had no union with her until she gave birth to a son. And he gave him the name Jesus. (1:18–20, 24–25)

Mary is clearly pregnant before they "came together." The child was conceived through the Holy Spirit. This description, along with Joseph's reaction to the whole episode, makes it obvious to any clear-minded reader what the intent of the record is. To argue that the New Testament record of the virgin birth is false is one thing; to argue that it does not teach a virgin birth or that the idea is an interpolation can only be done via a radical violation of the texts involved.

ARGUMENT FROM INFREQUENCY OF MENTION

It eventually became unfashionable to deny the virgin birth on the basis of the *alma–bethula* subtleties. One of the more modern bases for denial is on the grounds that the virgin birth is mentioned explicitly only twice in the New Testament. If such a miracle occurred, why isn't it mentioned in all the Gospels? Why doesn't Paul refer to it? On the basis of these questions, the conclusion is reached that the virgin birth was a fanciful story added to the record of Jesus' earthly life by Matthew and Luke.

Of the objections to the virgin birth, this seems the most remarkable. Those who confess that God is involved in the totality of the New Testament might ask how many times God must say something before it is believable. But of course those who follow this line of reasoning don't believe God can be the one doing the speaking. More to the point is a question of academic consistency. If we apply the principle of frequency of mention to other matters in the biblical record, we are left with a very abbreviated set of beliefs! Only Luke records the ascension of Jesus. Yet the whole concept of the lordship of Christ would be meaningless without his ascension. Mark begins his Gospel with the ministry of John the Baptist, saying nothing about the virgin birth. In fact, he says nothing about the birth of Jesus at all. Perhaps we can infer that Mark believed Jesus just appeared *de novo* on the scene of his baptism. To carry the principle further in our exercise of *reductio ad absurdum,* we must maintain that the virgin birth, though mentioned only twice, is cited by two different writers. While there may be some common sources that lie behind Matthew and Luke, their birth narratives are so different in style and viewpoint, how can their Gospels be considered a collaborative effort?

But what if only one author teaches a doctrine, though in multiple books? If Paul teaches a doctrine in ten texts, but it is taught by no one else, must that doctrine be scrapped? As a hermeneutical principle, how many times and by how many authors must a point be recorded before it can be considered an article of the Christian faith? The argument from infrequency of mention is simply too arbitrary. If the virgin birth were contradicted by other New Testament writers, then the question of frequency of mention would be relevant. That is not the case, so the argument is specious.

MYTHICAL PARALLELS

The skeptic appears to stand on more solid ground in collecting a series of pagan religious writings that allegedly tell a story similar to that of the birth of Christ. Here is a mythological motif that no religion of the day could be without. So the founders of this one, most likely Paul, who was educated in the pagan poets, brought their system into line.

In this frequent motif a god falls in love, or has a one-night stand, with a human. After their liaison, she becomes pregnant and eventually gives birth to a god-man-hero. The virgin birth then is seen as an intrusion into the biblical record by the heroes of Mount Olympus or from Ovid's *Metamorphosis.* There is, however, less here than meets the eye, and the argument rests on two shaky premises. First, it assumes too many parallels and overlooks radical differences in historiography between Gospel writers and Greek poets. To the Greek religious poet, it was unimportant whether miracles took place in history. Actual historical events had no bearing on their polytheistic religion. To the Hebrew, history was crucial.[1] The fundamental thesis of Hebrew religion was that Yahweh was the Creator and Lord of history, and history is therefore the sphere of his self-revelation. To see this contrast, one need only compare Luke with either Ovid or Homer, noting their differing ways of treating facts and their interpretation of events and the motives ascribed to the people and gods about whom they write.

Second, the argument is based on an elemental logical fallacy, the *post hoc ergo propter hoc* (after this, therefore, because of this) fallacy. That pagan narratives were written first does not add weight behind the premise that they influenced the New Testament writers. Evidence must develop the literary connection in other ways, and that connection is simply not possible to make through any kind of literary analysis.

If we apply the principle of pagan parallelism consistently, we face other critical theological problems. As Rudolf Bultmann has pointed out, pagan mythology not only included virgin birth stories, but also dying and rising gods. Thus, the resurrection is also suspect, though there is a long literary distance between Vulcan and Prometheus and the resurrected Jesus of Nazareth. Plato believed in God. That does not mean, however, that every subsequent theistic writer borrowed from him and is a Platonist. Such problems are endless. Selective comparisons that involve a vast oversimplification of historical witnesses must be avoided; they are useless.

Other arguments, including those of such theologians as Emil Brunner, have not received widespread support among higher critics. Certainly, answering objections to the virgin birth cannot confirm it by negation. But the purpose here is to show that the historicity of the virgin birth must be dealt with in the wider context of the reliability and trustworthiness of the entire biblical witness. One part of the narrative cannot be fairly judged in isolation.

The overarching concern of the New Testament is not the birth of a baby, but the incarnation of God. The Christian faith stands or falls with the incarnation. In the birth narratives, we have the climactic appearance in history of the long-awaited redeemer of Israel. In the incarnation, the *pleroma* occurs—the "fullness of time" arrives. This is not merely *a* fullness, but *the* fullness. This is the *kairotic* moment that is pregnant with meaning, a moment that is both historical and historic. The incarnation is the watershed not only of Western history, which is measured in terms of B.C. and A.D., but of all history. Here is the point of convergence among the Old Testament prophecies, the moment when light enters the world. This is where Yahweh "tents" (or "tabernacles," the exact translation of John 1:14) with his people. This is the scandal to the Greek, that the Word should become flesh. Thus, though the Gospel of John gives no report of the virgin birth, it is clear about what happens via the virgin birth. This is Scripture's own interpretation of the birth events:

> In the beginning was the Word, and the Word was with God, and the Word was God. He was with God in the beginning. Through him all things were made; without him nothing was made that has been made. In him was life, and that life was the light of men. The light shines in the darkness, but the darkness has not understood it. . . . The true light that gives light to every man was coming into the world. He was in the world, and though the world was made through him, the world did not recognize him. He came to that which was his own, but his own did not receive him. Yet to all who received him, to those who believed in his name, he gave the right to become children of God—children born not of natural descent, nor of human decision or a husband's will, but born of God. The Word became flesh and made his dwelling among us. We have seen his glory, the glory of the One and Only, who came from the Father, full of grace and truth. (John 1:1–14)

WHAT ABOUT MARY?

Protestants have missed something by treating Mary as if she had a communicable virus. The reason she seems a not-quite-honorable sister is our reaction to the excesses of the doctrines of immaculate conception, assumption, and other sorts of Mariolotry in the Catholic Church. The writers of the Apostles' Creed mention Mary by name, however. She is more than simply a handy surrogate mom. Mary should have our honor, not for her sake, but as the role model for a Christian, man or woman, par excellence.

Mary was chosen by God to make a total, radical, lifelong commitment. The choice was an act of grace that Mary neither sought nor deserved. Yet she had obviously been a young woman who desired to serve the living God. She was prepared to be a wife, mother, and whatever else God required. So when the time had come and she was asked to do the impossible, she paused at the sheer wonder of it all, then submitted herself completely. This is love for God and courage of the highest order. Her soul—and her heart and body—did indeed magnify the Lord.

Imagine the difficulties of raising her other children alongside a half brother who might disappear to debate theology with the temple leaders. This was her child and at the same time her Savior and Lord. Throughout Jesus' ministry we get hints that Mary is in the wings, supporting, fearing, praying, and perhaps witnessing to her unbelieving sons. She is available and faithful to the cross and beyond, never demanding the spotlight, always the obedient servant. It is idolatry to pray to Mary or to draw on her unhumanly righteousness from the treasury of merit.

But it is highly appropriate to pray to be like her in spirit.

RELATED RESOURCES
FROM LIGONIER MINISTRIES

John H. Gerstner. *Theology in Dialogue.*
R. C. Sproul. "Choosing My Religion," video or audio series, or book.
———. "Defending the Faith in a Faithless World," audio series.

————. *Essential Truths of the Christian Faith.*

————. "Mary," audio series.

————. *Mighty Christ.*

————. *Now, That's a Good Question.*

————. *The Glory of Christ.*

————. "The Life of Christ," video or audio series, and outline.

I believe . . .
in Jesus Christ, . . .
who . . . suffered under Pontius Pilate;
was crucified, dead, and buried;
he descended into hell.

Suffering Servant *for Me*

or years he has gone into prisons as a Christian witness, conducting services, leading Bible studies, discipling men. At the beginning he was struck by how much easier it was behind the walls and the fences for people to get over the barrier of self-righteousness to come to faith in Christ. There were plenty of problems in prison evangelism, but most inmates had a healthy sense that God had every right to be angry at them.

But my friend sees a change in that brokenness over the late 1980s and 1990s. More men and women inside prison have been "psychologized" out of their guilt. Maybe they committed the crime and they have to do the time, but they are not really "guilty." There are mental or emotional reasons for their weakness. They have a learning disorder that left them frustrated. The home environment was hell, and they were left with inner rage they could not control. They have done some unfortunate things, but they aren't *really* bad people. God should feel fortunate to have them on board if they decide to follow him.

This sort of thinking is hardly unique to the inmate population. What is frightening is that it is mirrored in our churches. Even within circles that are identified as "Bible-believing," a strong tendency has arisen to believe in universal atonement. Christ surely died for every person. If that is so, then the Bible's references to hell have been misunderstood. God will have some provision for bringing every person into heaven. Or those outside salvation will be annihilated.

It won't do. The Bible doesn't accept excuses for sin. Sinful human beings have no more place in the purity of heaven and the perfect holiness of God than do spiders on the rug of a five-star hotel.

Only if we accept the truth about ourselves and God's appropriate wrath at something so hideously evil can we truly know God's mercy. We must follow Jesus of Nazareth down the dirty streets of Jerusalem. But above all, to view gracious love lavished on the undeserving, we must stand at the foot of the cross.

> . . . He suffered under Pontius Pilate;
> was crucified, dead, and buried;
> He descended into hell . . .

Surely for this reason the Apostles' Creed leaps over the life of Jesus from his birth to his death. The work of the atonement would not have happened without a life of perfect obedience and submission to the Father. But that life, in the final analysis, sets the props onstage. The suffering of Christ stands at the core of classical Christianity. His passion occupies the central place, not only in the preaching and liturgy of the church, but in its music and visual art. The *Pieta* seeks to capture the climactic movement of the "great passion." The church understood that the death of Christ was the fruition of Jesus' mission.

A scandal to both Gentile and Jew, the suffering of Christ was intrinsic to his messianic vocation. Jesus expressed a compulsion for the task. He said the Son of Man *must* suffer many things. He set his face steadfastly toward Jerusalem. He assumed the role of the Suffering Servant of Israel who acquainted himself with grief and entered fully into the human predicament. Jesus moved inexorably toward his destiny to "drink the cup" the Father set before him.

HE SUFFERED

The Bible never regards suffering as an illusion, any more than it does the sin at its root. The Hebrew nation begins with the groans of an oppressed people and follows a consistent historical pattern of agony and pathos. Yet the Jews saw this suffering as an integral part of their covenantal destiny. Biblical faith accepts as a given the reality of the tragic. Physical and emotional pain do not come from a lower stratum of being, nor does Scripture flee into fanciful utopianism. Here is no fatalistic, tranquilizer-induced Stoicism, no theology of hopelessness. The consolation of Israel involves not a denial of suffering, but victory over it.

The only basis for Christian hope lies in the believer's participation in the *Man of Sorrows* and *Christus Victor*—the triumph of Christ. We become, in the words of Romans 8:37, "superconquerors" because of the suffering of Christ. Christian joy is not found in an existential leap into dialectical courage, but in an assurance that rests on historical reality.

Jesus did not say "Fear not" as a cosmic good-humor man who pats us on the back and tells us that everything is getting better and better in every way. Christ did not appeal to irrational sentimentality. Rather, the exhortation, "Fear not," is followed by a *reason:* "I have overcome the world" (John 16:33). This "overcoming" or "conquering" is accomplished via his suffering.

UNDER PONTIUS PILATE

Some have wondered why, of all the historical personages who surrounded Jesus, Pilate is given special consideration by the creed. This is no arbitrary assessment of guilt that elevates Pontius Pilate over Judas and Caiaphas in the hierarchy of sinners.[1] Rather, Pilate served a unique function in the historical unfolding of covenantal redemption.

Pilate represents the legal authority of the Gentile world. Jesus is tried and judged outside the camp. "Outside the camp" was the place of separation from the covenant for the people in the wilderness. Bull, heifer, and goat sin offerings were burned outside the camp (Exod. 29:14; Lev. 4:12, 21; 8:17; 9:11; 16:27; Num. 19:3, 9). Criminals were executed and blasphemers were buried there (Lev. 10:4–5; 24:14, 23; Num. 15:35–36). The unclean lived there through the time of their uncleanness (Lev. 13:46; 14:3; Num. 5:3–4; 12:14–15; 31:13, 19; Deut. 23:10). Outsiders remained there until they were accepted into the covenant community (Josh. 6:23). The writer of Hebrews makes this connection explicitly:

> The high priest carries the blood of animals into the Most Holy Place as a sin offering, but the bodies are burned outside the camp. And so Jesus also suffered outside the city gate to make the people holy through his own blood. Let us, then, go to him outside the camp, bearing the disgrace he bore. (Heb. 13:11–13)

Jesus is also delivered to the Gentiles, or the heathen, for judgment (Luke 24:7; Rom. 4:23). God had shown his covenant power and holiness in the Old Testament by delivering his people either from or into the hands of the Gentiles. Here we see the concurrence of secular history with the determined plan of redemptive history. Pilate acts as the executor of the authority and the will of imperial Rome; he also is the executor of the redemptive plan of God. Jesus says, somewhat enigmatically, "You would have no power over me if it were not given to you from above" (John 19:11).

WAS CRUCIFIED

That Jesus met his death by means of crucifixion has often been radically misunderstood by the church. The symbol of the cross has been virtually universal in Christendom. The meaning of that symbol has not.

To examine the significance of crucifixion, we must go beyond the traditional explanations that Jesus had to be put to death by Roman means because the Jews did not have the right of capital punishment under the juridical dominion of the Roman Empire. Had the Jews been free to execute, it would still have been necessary that Jesus die outside the context of Israel (see above). The meaning of the cross must be found within the framework of the redemptive history of Israel.

Paul relates the cross to the curse sanction of the Old Covenant, alluding to Deuteronomy 21:22–23:

> Christ redeemed us from the curse of the law by becoming a curse for us, for it is written: "Cursed is everyone who is hung on a tree." He redeemed us in order that the blessing given to Abraham might come to the Gentiles through Christ Jesus, so that by faith we might receive the promise of the Spirit. (Gal. 3:13–14)

Paul relates the cross to the blessing–curse motif of the Old Covenant. The concept of curse is strange and often confusing to the Western reader. The word *curse* gives rise to such images as the voudou practitioner who puts a "curse" on a victim by sticking pins in a doll of the victim's likeness. It is necessary to understand God's curse within the context of the covenant. The form of the Old Covenant followed that which was common in suzerainty treaties between kings and their vassals.[2] The covenant of Israel followed this Near Eastern pattern and included formulas of blessing and curse.[3] The blessing is on those who fulfill the stipulations of the covenant; the curse is laid on those who violate the stipulations.

Deuteronomy 27 outlines several curses that accompany specific violations of the law, ending with the general curse formula: "Cursed is the man who does not uphold the words of this law by carrying them out" (v. 26). Likewise, the blessing is promised to those who are obedient to the law:

> If you fully obey the LORD your God and carefully follow all his commands I give you today, the LORD your God will set you high above all the nations on earth. All these blessings will come upon you and accompany you if you obey the LORD your God. (Deut. 28:1–2)

The curse may be understood in contrast to blessing. To be blessed is the highest felicity of the Jew. Blessedness is not to be equated with ordinary happiness. Blessedness involves a transcendent dimension, a unique quality of happiness that is inseparably related to being in the presence of God and enjoying all the benefits that this involves. This may be illustrated partially by a glance at the Hebrew benediction: "The LORD bless you and keep you; the LORD make his face shine upon you and be gracious to you; the LORD turn his face toward you and give you peace" (Num. 6:24–26). In the benediction the elements of blessing (stated in parallels) include divine preservation, grace, and peace in the fullest sense of the word *shalom*. The presence of Yahweh in the midst of his tabernacle and temple was the concrete assurance of God's blessing.

To be cursed, then, is to be removed from the presence of God, to be set outside the camp, to be cut off from his benefits. The greatest terror to the Old Testament Jew was defilement—being pronounced "unclean" and driven out of the camp where the presence of God was focused. Adam and Eve suffered the curse when they were driven from the garden of Eden. The scapegoat of the Old Testament sacrificial system was driven out of the camp into the wilderness after the sins of the nation were symbolically imputed to it by the laying on of hands. This "separation" from the presence of God was symbolized by the covenant sign of circumcision. The covenant in the Old Testament was not said to be "written"; rather, it was "cut." In the rite of circumcision, the Jews bore not only the mark of ethnic separation, whereby they were set apart for holiness and blessedness, but also carried the sign of the curse where, by means of the rite, they declared, "May I be cut off from the presence of God and his benefits if I fail to keep the stipulations (the law) of the covenant."

On the cross, Jesus was cursed. He represented the covenant-breakers who were exposed to the curse and took the full measure of the curse upon himself. As the Lamb of God, the sin-bearer, he was cut off from the presence of God. On the cross, Jesus experienced forsakenness on our behalf. The darkness and earthquake that accompanied the event underscore the pain of the physical execution and focus on the loss of intimacy that the God-man Jesus enjoyed with God. God turned his back on Jesus and cut him off from all blessing, from all keeping, from all grace, and from all peace. Jesus did not die in the temple, but was killed outside the holy city at the hands of unclean Gentiles. Jesus was driven from the camp to experience the full horror of the unmitigated wrath of God. Nowhere in Scripture is the reality of God's wrath more sharply manifested than when he forsook his Messiah. Here, the negative sanction of circumcision was fulfilled. This is why Paul fought the Judaizers when they sought to reinstitute the religious significance of circumcision in the New Covenant community. For the Christian to receive circumcision as a religious rite was to repudiate its fulfillment on the cross and to place oneself once again under the curse of the Old Covenant law.

The meaning of the death of Christ cannot be exhausted by speaking of satisfaction and substitution. Theological explication will never totally penetrate the mystery that surrounds the cross. However, this event was not so enigmatic that we can say nothing meaningful about it at all. It is not enough to see the cross as an eloquent sermon on love or as the dramatic agony of an existential man. The New Testament pours considerable content regarding its *meaning* into the event. To ignore the content is to make the cross a chameleon that changes color with the surrounding theological foliage.

To avoid subjectivism and relativism, we must seek to understand the New Testament view of the cross. The crucifixion is inseparably related to Israel's national history and destiny. New Testament writers looked at the cross from the perspective of the Old Testament. Modern theologians who dismiss Paul's interpretation of the cross as an adaptation of Gnostic redeemer myths fail to recognize Paul's thoroughly Jewish background. John the Baptist's *Agnus Dei* quickly establishes this theme as he refers to Jesus as "the Lamb of God, who takes away the sin of the world" (John 1:29). From the beginning Jesus' mission is related to the Old Testament sacrificial system (Matt. 26:26–28). In the Epistle to the Hebrews, the relationship between the priestly office of Jesus and the levitical system of the Old Testament is given its fullest exposition. Jesus not only offers the perfect sacrifice for sins; he *is* the sacrifice. The superior character of this sacrifice is seen in that it was offered once for all (4:14–5:10; 6:19–20; 7:22–8:4; 9:11–14). Thus, the cross uniquely fulfills the Old Testament sacrificial system. Jesus is the absolute oblation in that he lays down his life for his sheep (John 10:15–17).

This principle of atonement as reconciliation between God and human is related most significantly to the Suffering Servant of Isaiah 53. That the New Testament community found its rationale for the cross in this Old Testament context cannot be disputed. According to the witness of Luke, the risen Jesus himself explains the cross via the Old Testament. In his postresurrection appearance on the road to Emmaus, he admonished:

> "How foolish you are, and how slow of heart to believe all that the prophets have spoken! Did not the Christ have to suffer these things and then enter his glory?" And beginning with Moses and all the Prophets, he explained to them what was said in all the Scriptures concerning himself. (Luke 24:25–27)

The issue in the church today is whether we take these words seriously. Is Jesus the Incarnate One who acts in history to bring about cosmic redemption, or is this only an existential myth that speaks to us subjectively in the here and now? This is no mere intramural squabble among theologians; it has life-and-death importance. It reflects something of the classic struggle between the temple and the academy, between Abraham and Plato. The theologian often neglects the question: "If the Jesus of history is not known accurately via the New Testament, why should we be concerned about him at all?" The church asserts through the Apostles' Creed that the New Testament understanding of the cross is not a mythical creation. It is the truly risen Lord's accurate interpretation of a historical event. If the biblical view is the fraud of primitive Christianity, it is too late now to reconstruct a dying Jesus who is authentic. Without the biblical interpretation of the meaning of the cross, we are left to discover its meaning by individual subjective approaches to the event. If that is the case, we are left with a meaningless cross and an irrelevant kerygma or message.

The ramifications of the atonement are difficult enough to keep the most erudite scholar busily engaged for a lifetime. Yet even a child can understand the basic concept. The church must guard against falling unwittingly into the Gnostic trap of making the gospel understandable only to the intellectual elite. Reconciliation is not limited to those who can master contemporary existential philosophy as a prerequisite for understanding the meaning of Christ.

DEAD AND BURIED

The theme of the "blood" of Jesus is prominent in popular hymnody. This has occasioned much misunderstanding. The English folksinger-evangelist, John Guest, once raised the question:

"If Jesus merely had scratched his finger on a nail, would that have been enough?" Guest was pointing out that a scratch produces blood but rarely is it fatal. Scripture's view of the blood of Christ is a graphic image of life and death. The blood of Jesus is the pouring out of his life in the throes of death.

In biblical categories, death is ultimately related to sin. Death is the final curse of the law. The root of this is found in the prohibition given to the first man at creation: "You are free to eat from any tree in the garden; but you must not eat from the tree of the knowledge of good and evil, for when you eat of it you will surely die" (Gen. 2:16–17). In this warning, the gift of life is forfeited by transgression. Hans Küng pointed out that the judgment of death is not given "in general," but the full penalty suggests *immediate* death. "When you eat of it you will surely die." Küng writes:

> Sacred scripture sees death in connection with sin, and it presents this truth without glossing over it. Thus in sin the sinner earns for himself instantaneous death—instantaneous death in the massive Old Testament body-soul sense of the word. The sinner does "deserve to die."[4]

In the covenant of creation, sin is a capital offense. That God does not enact the penalty immediately is an indication of his grace. In the Old Covenant, God further expressed grace by restricting capital punishment to a limited list of major offenses. By cultural comparison with today's standards, the Old Testament list of capital offenses seems severe. Yet in the total perspective of the covenant of creation, the Old Testament is a history, not of severity, but of God's continual, long-suffering mercy to his covenant-violating, life-forfeiting people. From time to time in biblical history, the people of God are given sober reminders of the divine prerogatives of judgment, as in the case of Uzzah, who touched the ark of the covenant, or Ananias and Sapphira, who lied to the Holy Spirit.

Once we grasp the gravity of sin and its destructive power, we may gain better insight into the grace of God as he operates in history. Without an understanding of sin and the holiness of God, the Old Testament, as well as the cross, will remain a scandal.

Jesus died. In death, he received judgment. The One who was obedient was stricken with the judgment of the disobedient. The judgment of the first Adam was transferred to the second Adam. The life of the second Adam was given to the descendants of the first Adam. The sting of death was removed.

G. C. Berkouwer writes that the death of a Christian is "no longer a payment for sin but is now simply a transfer from sin to eternal life."[5] In baptism, the Christian identifies with, and vicariously participates in, the death of Christ. The transfer to life is not effected because Jesus bled, but because his bleeding was to death.

The burial of Jesus has far more significance than is accorded in the liturgy and devotional life of the church. The burial actually becomes a radical point of departure in the general progression of the work of Christ from humiliation to exaltation. Its significance cannot be limited to being an external proof of the reality of death or the sanctification of the Christian practice of burying the dead. Rather, the true significance of the burial is indicated in the conditions and circumstances surrounding it. Luke's account of the burial reads as follows:

> Now there was a man named Joseph, a member of the Council, a good and upright man, who had not consented to their decision and action. He came from the Judean town of Arimathea and he was waiting for the kingdom of God. Going to Pilate, he asked for Jesus' body. Then he took it down, wrapped it in linen cloth and placed it in a tomb cut in the rock, one in which no one had yet been laid. It was Preparation Day, and the Sabbath was about to begin. The women who had come with Jesus from Galilee followed Joseph and saw the tomb and how his body was laid in it. Then they went home and prepared spices and perfumes. But they rested on the Sabbath in obedience to the commandment. (Luke 23:50–56)

Matthew adds to the description of Joseph of Arimathea the adjectival qualifier *rich* (Matt. 27:57). That Jesus was buried in the elegance of the rich stood in sharp contrast to the customary procedure of disposing of the bodies of executed criminals. The body of Jesus was not dumped unceremoniously on the garbage heap outside Jerusalem. It was treated with honor and respect. To the Jew, such treatment is important. Consider the Old Testament history regarding the death and burial of the patriarchs. Abraham's grave was a prime possession. Joseph's bones were carried out of Egypt into the land of promise. Moses, the mediator of the Old Covenant, was buried secretly by Yahweh himself. That the Messiah received a dignified burial signified the end of humiliation and the beginning of exaltation. The ignominy of forsakenness was over. On the cross, Jesus commended his spirit to the care of the Father. From that moment, his body was no longer subject to degradation.

The material circumstance of Jesus' burial was its literal fulfillment of the predicted destiny of Isaiah's Suffering Servant:

> He was assigned a grave with the wicked, and with the rich in his death, though he had done no violence, nor was any deceit in his mouth. (Isa. 53:9)

In the irony of fulfillment, Jesus is first numbered with the wicked, dying like a criminal in the company of criminals, yet he gains the burial of the rich. This, in the context of the prophecy, is a positive, rather than a negative, factor.

DESCENDED INTO HELL

The statement in the Apostles' Creed that Jesus descended into hell is often attended by an asterisk. Some communions avoid the problem by leaving this phrase out. A footnote is helpful to explain this problematic phrase. At best there is a disagreement as to its meaning between the classic Roman Catholic understanding and that of Protestants. Roman Catholic and Lutheran theologians have tended to view the descent of Christ into hell as a mission of victory and liberation. The classic proof text for this view is 1 Peter 3:18–20a:

> For Christ died for sins once for all, the righteous for the unrighteous, to bring you to God. He was put to death in the body but made alive by the Spirit, through whom also he went and preached to the spirits in prison who disobeyed long ago when God waited patiently in the days of Noah while the ark was being built.

The preaching to the "spirits in prison" is regarded as an allusion to an alleged ministry that took place between the hour of Christ's death and the moment of his resurrection.

Some difficulty attends this theory, inasmuch as the Petrine text is somewhat ambiguous as to the identity of the spirits in prison and unclear as to the time when this preaching took place. The problem is heightened by the fact that other New Testament texts strongly suggest that Jesus was elsewhere between his death and resurrection. Two statements on the cross seem to demand that Jesus was with the Father in heaven. First, Jesus says to the thief at his side, "I tell you the truth, today you will be with me in paradise" (Luke 23:43). The punctuation of this passage can be changed so it reads, "I tell you the truth today, you will be with me in paradise." The latter rendition is less likely on grammatical grounds, though not impossible. Second, at the moment of his death, Jesus said, "Father, into your hands I commit my spirit" (Luke 23:46). Having the spirit of Jesus in the presence of the Father at the same time he is on a preaching mission to hell raises some serious problems.

The theological issue at stake is, Did Jesus experience the full penalty for sin, namely, punishment in hell? To descend to hell in punishment would be a far different purpose than to go there to proclaim victory to the dead. It also calls into question the statement of Luke 16:26 that, between heaven and hell, "a great chasm has been fixed, so that those who want to go from here to you cannot, nor can anyone cross over from there to us." When all the evidence is considered, it seems quite improbable that Jesus literally descended into hell.

So why say it? As they contemplated the statement, John Calvin and some of the other Reformers considered that this phrase does indeed make a great and true confession—though perhaps not the one the original writers had in view. Calvin and others define that descent as the spiritual reality of Jesus' soul while he hung rejected and condemned by his Father on the cross. To be forsaken, to be cut off by God, brings with it the full torment of hell.

The New Testament is as clear as is Isaiah 53 that Jesus did take on himself the Christian's earned spot in hell. He accomplished the active obedience and punitive suffering necessary to secure redemption of all who believe and confess. All was finished by Jesus, the Suffering Servant of Israel.

RELATED RESOURCES
FROM LIGONIER MINISTRIES

John H. Gerstner. "The Way of Salvation," audio series and outline.

Martin Luther. *The Bondage of the Will.*

R. C. Sproul. "A Shattered Image," video or audio series, and study guide.

———. *Commentary on Romans.*

———. "Dealing with Difficult Romans," video or audio series, and outline.

———. "Roman Catholicism," audio series.

———. "Romans Interact," audio series and study notebook.

———. "Surprised by Suffering," video or audio series, or book.

———. "The Atonement of Jesus," audio series.

———. "The Cross of Christ," video or audio series, and study guide.

———. "The Drama of Redemption," audio series.

———. "The Holiness of God," video or audio series, or book.

———. "The Sacrifice of Faith," video.

———. "Themes from Romans," video or audio series.

I believe . . .
the third day he arose again
from the dead.

8

Grave with a View

If the twentieth century has choked on the virgin birth, modern theologians have tried to apply the Heimlich maneuver to dislodge the resurrection of Christ. In this our generation is not alone. Twice the New Testament records that Paul ran into prejudice against the resurrection: among intellectuals who heard his Mars Hill sermon and among the Jewish Sadducees. But at the time of the first proclamation of the gospel, the most serious intellectual stumbling block to the Greeks was not so much the resurrection as the incarnation. They could not comprehend this humiliation of God. Modern hearers don't seem to mind a humiliated Christ. Proclaim the resurrection, however, and rationalists head for the door. There has never been a time when the resurrection was so thoroughly questioned and so critically analyzed as it is today—and it is happening within the church.

WANTED, DEAD AND ALIVE

The resurrection is now firmly denied within the Christian church by a multitude of clergy and academicians. Rudolf Bultmann's theology has captured *acceptable* theological scholarship. Bultmann said:

> All our thinking today is shaped irrevocably by modern science. A blind acceptance of the New Testament mythology would be arbitrary, and to press for its acceptance as an article of faith would be to reduce faith to works. . . . Man's knowledge and mastery of the world have advanced to such an extent through science and technology that it is no longer possible for anyone seriously to hold the New Testament view of the world—in fact, there is no one who does. . . . The miracles of the New Testament have ceased to be miraculous, and to defend their historicity by recourse to nervous disorders or hypnotic effects only serves to underline the fact. . . . It is impossible to use electric light and the wireless and to avail ourselves of modern medical and surgical discoveries, and at the same time to believe in the New Testament world of spirits and miracles. We may think we can manage it in our own lives, but to expect others to do so is to make the Christian faith unintelligible and unacceptable to the modern world.[1]

On the third day He rose again from the dead.

Bultmann finds it inconceivable that a twentieth-century sophisticate, who understands the natural laws of the universe, might accept a physical resurrection. Bultmann and modern theologians speak of the risen Christ, but the resurrection did not happen in historical time and space. The resurrection is a myth. Jesus Christ died, is dead, and will remain dead. Yet we still can say that God raised Jesus.

Modern theology thrives on this contradiction. At one time, theological statements that violated the law of contradiction would be regarded as nonsense. Quite the opposite is now the case. No wonder Christianity has a credibility problem among thinking unbelievers! The "post-Christian generation" did not abandon the church so much because they were too sophisticated to believe in the resurrection. Rather, it is silly to join a church that believes nothing except illogical spiritual double-talk. It wasn't that the baby boomers who came to adulthood in the 1960s and 1970s were too strung out on pot to listen when they attended their parents' liberal churches. The problem is that they *were* listening. Now their children have reached adulthood, ready to fall prey to philosophies far more unbelievable than Christianity.

All this leaves us to wonder how rationalism drove the church into irrationality. The reason has to do with dialectic thinking that glues the philosophy of existentialism to religion. A *dialectic* is a tension between incompatible contradictory ideas. The dialectic method attempts to see truth in both polarities at the same time. The goal is that a *thesis* and an *antithesis* might coalesce as a *synthesis*. As a result, the law of noncontradiction was quite irrelevant to Bultmann in his search for existential spiritual "faith" to replace the orthodox Christianity he could not accept. In a historical sense, Jesus of Nazareth is dead, yet in the faith community he remains alive. A person sitting outside the garden tomb on Easter morning would have seen nothing amiss. Yet we can still confess that God raised Jesus from the dead in us. Note in the quotation above that Bultmann charges those who insist on faith in an actual resurrection with following a works righteousness. *Real* faith, he believes, has no such absolutes. Faith can demand nothing of us except an existentialist leap into irrationality.

This line of thinking is really quite remarkable when one thinks it through. The resurrection did not happen; it is a myth. That does not, however, make it unimportant. The fact that the early church proclaimed and urged people to submit to such mythology *is* historical fact. The fact that people preached such nonsense underlies the *importance* they attached to their understanding of the historical Jesus. So the myth is important, insofar as we see that myths sprang up around the person of Jesus, and people must have gotten meaning from those myths. Jesus of Nazareth is no more than a historical curiosity, but this religious impulse, which does seem to persist, holds meaning for humanity. We need to know what these deluded believers learned from the man Jesus and what we can learn from this man today. That which we can learn we will call *Christianity*.

There is one objective reality to grab hold of here—the early church and its *kerygma* or proclamation. But in the one place existential theology allows a historical foundation, it doesn't accord with the facts. Literary criticism and discoveries of manuscript fragments have firmly anchored the New Testament to the first century.[2] That should make Bultmannian scholars exceedingly uncomfortable, because their theories demand a significant passage of time during which real history evolves into myth and legend. The Bible testifies that the early church immediately owned a fully developed and cogent *kerygma,* the essential proclamation of the gospel. When the apostles went out to preach, they used words and spoke in meaningful sentences that can be analyzed by rules of grammar. They were not locked into a rationalistic system, but they did speak reasonably. Without question, thousands and thousands became convinced of the truth of their statements. These people were not acquainted with nuclear fission, but they knew how the world works. They certainly didn't go to their neighbors and say that Jesus Christ is risen and is still dead.

The first public proclamation of the resurrection was on the day of Pentecost, when Peter stated a fact, made an assertion, and gave a reason for his assertion. He told the crowd:

> Jesus of Nazareth was a man accredited by God to you by miracles, wonders and signs, which God did among you through him, as you yourselves know. This man was handed over to you by God's set purpose and foreknowledge; and you, with the help of wicked men, put him to death by nailing him to the cross. But God raised him from the dead, freeing him from the agony of death, because it was impossible for death to keep its hold on him. (Acts 2:22–24)

As in the case of the virgin birth, if this is a closed universe, in which it is impossible for anything to transcend natural law, then Bultmann is right. A resurrection is manifestly impossible. But is that the only possibility for rational people? Bultmann does not support his proposition that every thinking person knows that miracles are impossible. He simply demands that we accept what he says or be excluded from the ranks of rational humanity.

If the possibility of an open universe is admitted—and Bultmann cannot disprove the possibility of an open universe—then all his confident assertions sound like bravado. Speaking from the assumption of an open universe, Peter said that it was impossible that death should hold One who is uniquely in such communion with God, so anointed by God, and of such intrinsic holiness. The apostles thought it irrational to assume that Jesus would stay dead. Their difference with Bultmann is one of conflicting worldviews.[3] In the open universe worldview, natural laws are simply how God normally operates the cosmos. But a creator God is *always* in control. The laws are his. The resurrection can be described as a miracle. A miracle does not break an immutable law in an open universe. A miracle in the New Testament sense is extraordinary, different from the normal course of affairs. It is considered normal in the twentieth century that dead people stay in the grave. The same could be said of the first century. But the resurrection of Jesus was not normal.

"God has raised him from the dead" was an astounding statement that lies at the heart of the New Testament *kerygma.* In the resurrection, God vindicates Jesus.

THE MOST IMPORTANT MESSAGE

Today, truth is often determined relativistically. That is why a dialectic is possible. The content or object of a person's faith is not important. The contemporary credo is: "Believing is important." To New Testament Christians, the object of faith was preeminent. Many individuals throughout history have claimed to represent the *only* true religion. By contrast, our pluralistic society says that it doesn't matter what one believes as long as it works. But only one person in history has had the ultimate sign of authenticity— resurrection from the dead. Thus, the apostle Peter points to David's words in the Old Testament:

> I have set the LORD always before me.
> Because he is at my right hand,
> I will not be shaken.
> Therefore my heart is glad and my tongue rejoices;
> my body also will rest secure,
> because you will not abandon me to the grave,
> nor will you let your Holy One see decay.
> You have made known to me the path of life;
> you will fill me with joy in your presence,
> with eternal pleasures at your right hand. (Ps. 16:8–11)

The Old Testament interpreters, the rabbinic scholars in the Talmud and other places, interpreted this passage in the Psalms to mean that David was speaking about himself. Peter says David may have been talking partly about his soul, but he was not the "Holy One." David was dead and buried. A first-century tour guide could point out his sepulcher. David could not have been referring to himself when he said that God would not let his *body* decay, that his bones are dust:

> Brothers, I can tell you confidently that the patriarch David died and was buried, and his tomb is here to this day. But he was a prophet and knew that God had promised him on oath that he would place one of his descendants on his throne. Seeing what was ahead, he spoke of the resurrection of the Christ, that he was not abandoned to the grave, nor did his body see decay.

God has raised this Jesus to life, and we are all witnesses of the fact. (Acts 2:29–32)

Not long afterward, when Peter and John met a lame man begging, Peter healed him in the authority of Jesus of Nazareth (Acts 3:6–7). When people gathered to learn what had happened, Peter connected his act with Jesus' resurrection: "Know this, you and all the people of Israel: It is by the name of Jesus Christ of Nazareth, whom you crucified but whom God raised from the dead, that this man stands before you healed" (Acts 4:10). It was not Peter's power that raised the man from his crippled condition. It was the power of the risen Christ.

In the New Testament, the reality of the resurrection of Jesus Christ stands at the heart of the preaching of the early church. First Corinthians 15 is the greatest defense of the resurrection found in Scripture. In Corinth there were "Bultmanns" who wanted to dehistoricize the resurrection. They were saying that Jesus had not really come back from the dead. Paul pins these people to the wall: "Now, brothers, I want to remind you of the gospel I preached to you, which you received and on which you have taken your stand. By this gospel you are saved, if you hold firmly to the word I preached to you. Otherwise, you have believed in vain" (vv. 1–2).

In 1 Corinthians 15, Paul thinks things through logically and considers the implications if the resurrection is not a real space–time event. If resurrection is impossible, then the only logical conclusion is the same as Bultmann's: that Christ is not risen.[4] However, Paul warns, understand that "if Christ has not been raised, our preaching is useless." Preaching was important to the teaching and interpretation of the words of Jesus. If there was no preaching, there was no Christ-following community. But not only is preaching vain, but "so is your faith." Christian faith has both object and content. It indeed involves an emotional response and a favorable disposition of the heart, but it also involves intellectual assent to historical reality.

As far as that aspect of it is concerned, if Christ is not risen their faith is meaningless. It also follows, says Paul, that "we are found to be false witnesses about God, for we have testified about God that he raised Christ from the dead." Not only is our preaching futile; it is sinful, because we're lying when we tell people that God has raised up Jesus, if that is really not true.

"And if Christ has not been raised, your faith is futile; you are still in your sins. . . . If only for this life we have hope in Christ, we are to be pitied more than all men" (vv. 13–19). Understandably, the apostle remonstrates: "And as for us, why do we endanger ourselves every hour? I die every day—I mean that, brothers—just as surely as I glory over you in Christ Jesus our Lord" (vv. 30–31). If, after all I have gone through and suffered for Christ's sake, it is worthless because there is no resurrection, Paul says, I might as well join the Epicureans with their philosophy of "eat, drink, and be merry, for tomorrow we die." If Christ isn't raised, then *death* is the true meaning of human existence.

The issue, as Paul sees it, is "either-or." Forget the dialectical "sort-of-both-and." Either life is meaningful, or it is not, and there can be meaning only if something follows life. If life ends in annihilation, then ultimate reality is the grave. If there is no resurrection, we can have no pretensions of human significance. Paul is not arguing that we should believe in the resurrection of Christ because it gives hope and meaning. He merely draws out the implications if the reality of resurrection is falsified.

Paul leaves no middle ground between resurrection and meaninglessness. He attacks all positions between faith in the resurrection and nihilism. Fortunately, we don't have to believe in spite of evidence to the contrary or because we fear meaningless life: "For what I received I passed on to you as of first importance: that Christ died for our sins according to the Scriptures, that he was buried, that he was raised on the third day according to the Scriptures" (1 Cor. 15:3–4).[5] Don't forget that Paul was a Jew, and the Jews had come to recognize that the Scriptures could be trusted as firm truth. Time after time the Scriptures had been proven to hold firmly to reality. Jesus rose *according to the Scriptures*. If no other reason should compel us to believe in the resurrection of Christ than this, it should be enough. The prophets said it would happen, and it did.

But Paul also appeals to empirical evidence:

> And that he appeared to Peter, and then to the Twelve. After that, he appeared to more than five hundred of the brothers at the same time, most of whom are still living, though some have fallen asleep. Then he appeared to James, then to all the apostles, and last of all he appeared to me also, as to one abnormally born. (1 Cor. 15:5–8)

With his own eyes and ears, he saw and heard the risen Christ, as did many others. Peter says the same thing in 2 Peter 1:16: "We did not follow cleverly invented stories when we told you about the power and coming of our Lord Jesus Christ, but we were eyewitnesses of his majesty."

A SAFE PLACE OF TRUTH

Death remains a frightening unknown, the monster under the bed when the lights go out. The process of dying often requires courage and fortitude. But the child can feel better intellectually in the reassurance of parents who are asleep in the next room. They are stronger than the child's fears. I may feel some remaining trepidation about the process of dying. Death remains the enemy of sinful human beings. But intellectually I know that death has become a safe place. In Christ, God confronted the grave on its own turf—and won. Christ is the firstborn from among the dead (Col. 1:18), the firstfruits of those who have fallen asleep (1 Cor. 15:26, 54–57). Paul shouts that Jesus has been there and conquered, just as he will conquer all other powers of the dark (1 Cor. 15:24–25)—"For he must reign."

Therefore, "Stand firm. Let nothing move you. Always give yourselves fully to the work of the Lord, because you know that your labor in the Lord is not in vain" (1 Cor. 15:58). The certainty that labor is not futile is inseparably related to the appearance in time and space of the resurrected Jesus. This knowledge is not a mystical insight or psychological wish-projection. We have the testimony of credible eyewitnesses.

RELATED RESOURCES FROM LIGONIER MINISTRIES

R. C. Sproul. "Abortion," video or audio series, and study guide.
———. "Chosen by God," video or audio series, and study guide, or book.
———. "Ecclesiastes," audio series.
———. "Heaven," audio series.
———. "If God Is Good, Why Do I Suffer?" video or audio message.
———. "Joy," audio series.
———. "Predestination," audio series.
———. "The City of God," audio series.
———. "Themes from Ecclesiastes," video or audio series.
———. *Vanity and Meaning.*
———. "Worldviews in Conflict," audio series.

I believe . . .
he ascended into heaven,
and sits at the right hand
of God the Father Almighty.

9

There for Us

Which event is most important: The incarnation? The crucifixion? The resurrection? This question has no final answer, for these events are interrelated and interdependent. The cross is meaningless without the incarnation and incomplete without the resurrection. Less central to Christian thought is the return of Christ to heaven at the end of his earthly ministry. Yet that, too, is part of the whole plan of God, so vital that none of the other events makes sense without it. The ascension is not only the culmination of New Testament history, but also the focal point of much Old Testament prophecy.

Actually, Roman Catholics have paid appropriate attention to the ascension. Observance of Ascension Day and Pentecost has not figured prominently in the Protestant calendar. Their celebration is overwhelmed by Christmas and Easter. Even Reformation Day is celebrated more festively. This oversight is unfortunate. The significance of the ascension and Pentecost seems to be vastly underestimated in the Protestant community.

The ascension is important because it is an essential element of the kingdom of God, and there is no more important theme in the Old and New Testaments. This kingdom reaches its zenith in the coronation of Jesus as the eternal Messiah-King. Jesus cannot be King without the ascension. Thus, the ascension cannot be an insignificant postscript. It is supremely important, as Jesus told his disciples at the Last Supper:

> I have told you this, so that when the time comes you will remember that I warned you. I did not tell you this at first because I was with you. Now I am going to him who sent me, yet none of you asks me, "Where are you going?" Because I have said these things, you are filled with grief. But I tell you the truth: It is for your good that I am going away. Unless I go away, the Counselor will not come to you; but if I go, I will send him to you. When he comes, he will convict the world of guilt in regard to sin and righteousness and judgment: in regard to sin, because men do not believe in me; in regard to righteousness, because I am going to the Father, where you can see me no longer; and in regard to judgment, because the prince of this world now stands condemned. (John 16:4–11)

> . . . He Ascended into Heaven
> and Sits at the Right Hand of God the Father almighty . . .

This is only one allusion by Jesus to his departure. It was cryptic and left the disciples in bewildered sorrow. Jesus discerned their emotions and stated that his departure was to their benefit. Jesus was making a value judgment that his absence would be necessary if better things were to come. That Jesus' absence is in any sense "better" than his incarnational presence has always been difficult for the church to grasp. Christians daydream about how glorious it would be to sit at Jesus' feet on the mountainside, to see as concrete reality what the Old Testament prophets could only glimpse in their imagination. Yet our situation is better than the fellowship with Jesus that the disciples enjoyed. Whatever privileges they knew at the time of Jesus' sojourn on earth, they were still in the context of pre-ascension history, which was less glorious.

Even the disciples came to realize that the ascension was not an occasion for lament. The historical account reads:

When he had led them out to the vicinity of Bethany, he lifted up his hands and blessed them. While he was blessing them, he left them and was taken up into heaven. Then they worshiped him and returned to Jerusalem with great joy. And they stayed continually at the temple, praising God. (Luke 24:50–53)

This narrative closes the Gospel of Luke. What an unexpectedly joyous finale, inasmuch as Luke records the departure of Jesus. That is surprising and significant when one thinks about it. While the ascension was not a moment that called for despair, it was a moment of separation. We know from experience that sorrow usually accompanies such separation. The disciples felt immense sorrow when Jesus announced that he would be going away.

Obviously, something had changed the disciples' perceptions since the initial announcement. New insight enabled them to rejoice, even as they lost sight of their master and friend. We need to draw on their understanding for the contemporary church.

JESUS IN SESSION

The New Testament makes clear that the ascension is pivotal. Its importance, however, extends beyond the mere facts of the event. Its significance must be seen in its relationship to the "session" of Christ at the right hand of God the Father and to the sending of the Holy Spirit on Pentecost.

To ascend in biblical categories is not merely to "go up." To be sure, the word *ascend* (Greek *anabaino*) is commonly used in the New Testament in this way. It also takes on cultic significance, in that people "go up" to Jerusalem to worship and even a spiritual significance with ascent of the soul to heaven. But in connection with the work of the Messiah, the word has a technical use. It has to do with going up, not to heaven in general, but to the throne of

God in particular. Jesus' work of atonement is finished. He, therefore, goes up to heaven and sits at the place of cosmic authority beside God the Father. Jesus reigns exalted as cosmic King, with a unique position in the kingdom of God. No one else "ascends" into heaven like this.[1]

The ascension culminates in the "session." At the right hand of the Father, Jesus assumes authority over the world. In this exalted position, Jesus is crowned King of kings and Lord of lords. All authority on heaven and earth rests in his hands. While Jesus' kingdom is not *of* this world, his reign ultimately extends *over* this world.

This does not separate the reign of Christ from earthly matters. On the contrary, it brings earthly powers and authority structures into inescapable relationship with Christ.

THE BASIS FOR HUMAN AUTHORITY

The fact of Christ's status of cosmic King mandates the Christian to an unusually high regard for earthly spheres of authority. Paul, for example, exhorts slaves to obey their masters and citizens to respect the power of civil authorities—even those that are obviously corrupt (Rom. 13:1–7; Eph. 6:5; Col. 3:22; Titus 2:9). Peter exhorts: "Submit yourselves for the Lord's sake to every authority instituted among men: whether to the king, as the supreme authority, or to governors, who are sent by him to punish those who do wrong and to commend those who do right" (1 Peter 2:13–14).

This frequent admonition to submission to earthly rulers has caused consternation to many Christians. It often seems inconsonant with the disciples' own behavior. Peter and John defied the Sanhedrin's prohibition to preach with their rhetorical proposition: "Judge for yourselves whether it is right in God's sight to obey you rather than God" (Acts 4:19). The whole question of civil obedience has frequently touched the raw nerves of society. What about tax moneys that are used for immoral purposes? What about obedience to restraining orders against protest at abortion clinics or zoning ordinances that prohibit gathering for neighborhood prayer and Bible study? What about laws that legitimize homosexual "marriages" and force Christian employers to provide spouse benefits to illicit lovers? What about unfair regulation of evangelism or Christian day and home schools? Such controversies have always been part of Christian relationships with government. Certainly this is no mere academic discussion in our own time.

The basic principle in the New Testament is clear: We ought to obey the civil authority unless the civil authority commands us to do that which God forbids or forbids us from doing that which God commands. Then we *must* disobey. The principle is easy; the application is often complex. Though the New Testament leaves room for civil disobedience and gives no simplistic categorical imperatives for obedience in every situation, there is a strong undercurrent of concern that Christians be models of civic responsibility in civil obedience. Paul's exhortation to slaves to obey their masters did not sanction slavery as a legitimate human institution. To the contrary, the rationale for the abolition of this exploitative practice is clearly present in the New Testament.[2] But we can see that God has neither commanded the individual to seek freedom, nor prohibited Christians from accepting oppression or slavery. Rather, we have been called to participate in the humiliation of Christ to bring honor to the exalted Christ.

Unfortunately, disobedience frequently arises from a feeling of superiority and self-righteousness over unbelievers. It threatens to damage witness to Christ, even as it complicates society's proper role in dealing with lawlessness. If Christians think they must break laws, the abundance of admonitions in the New Testament to the contrary serves as a caution. The apostolic attitude is: Obey civil authorities when you possibly can without betraying Christ. Peter calls us to do this for the Lord's sake.

How, then, can civil behavior have a bearing on our relationship with the Lord? The New Testament seems concerned about the proper recognition and exaltation of the authority of Christ. A cosmic dimension of lawlessness exists in the world. Authorities of this world will be sharply judged for their refusal to submit to the authority of Christ. All authority may be traced indirectly to the ultimate authority that resides in the office of Christ. An earthly ruler who fails to rule in conformity with Christ participates in the spirit of cosmic lawlessness, in the spirit of Antichrist. The Christian in such a world is called to be different whenever possible. Christians are to stimulate peace, not add to lawlessness. By submission the Christian participates in the humiliation of Christ, endures patient suffering, and bears witness to a spirit of obedience that authorities often lack. Submission testifies to the reality of the reign of Christ, whom we are to exalt by our obedience.

The right hand of God is the seat of ultimate authority. This position is occupied by the One God has anointed King. It is both a royal and a judicial position. Christ is installed as Judge at the supreme tribunal. Yet, paradoxically, the Judge is also Mediator. Christ is at once Judge and Advocate, Prosecutor and Defense Attorney. The account of the martyrdom of Stephen demonstrates this dual role:

> When they heard this, they were furious and gnashed their teeth at him. But Stephen, full of the Holy Spirit, looked up to heaven and saw the glory of God, and Jesus standing at the right hand of God. "Look," he said, "I see heaven open and the Son of Man standing at the right hand of God." At this they covered their ears and, yelling at the top of their voices, they all rushed at him, dragged him out of the city and began to stone him. (Acts 7:54–58a)

As Stephen is condemned by the ruling council of Israel, he has a vision of Jesus, *standing* at the right hand of God. To be seated at the right hand is to be in the position of judge. The defense attorney stands in the courtroom, not the judge. In the vision, Stephen glimpses the mediatorial work of Christ. As the Sanhedrin condemns Stephen to death, the ascended Christ rises to defend him. Thus, in ascension we receive not only an exalted King, but also One who is our ultimate Mediator.

THE BASIS FOR INTERCESSION

In biblical categories, the ascent into heaven is not limited to Jesus' elevation to divine kingship. There is also the dimension of ascending and entering the Holy of Holies as an ultimate priest. Jesus ascends not only to royalty, but also to the position of Intercessor as great High Priest. Thus, Christ ascends to the role of King-Priest. These offices, which were separate in the Old Covenant, are united in the New Covenant in the person of Christ.

Unlike the high priest of Israel, who was the only one who could enter the Holy of Holies once a year, Christ takes up residence in the ultimate Holy of Holies and involves himself in a perpetual ministry of intercession. He fulfills the prophecy of the King who is also the Priest forever after the order of Melchizedek. The psalmist wrote:

> The LORD says to my Lord: "Sit at my right hand until I make your enemies a footstool for your feet." . . . The LORD has sworn and will not change his mind: "You are a priest forever, in the order of Melchizedek." (Ps. 110:1, 4; see also Gen. 14:18–20; Heb. 5, 9, 10)

That Jesus occupies the office of Intercessor should console the Christian immensely. On a human level, people feel a greater sense of expectancy in matters of prayer when particular people are praying for them. The historical development in the Roman Catholic

Church of seeking the intercession of departed saints in general, and Mary in particular, may be rooted in this desire for intercessors whose prayers are effective. The apostle James instructs us that "the prayer of a righteous man is powerful and effective" (5:16b). This is good news and an encouragement to prayer until we discover that we are not so righteous. Hence we commonly seek those we regard as more righteous than ourselves to pray for us. Herein is the consolation of the Christian, that the efficacy of the prayers of Christ are available. The author of Hebrews declares:

> Therefore, since we have a great high priest who has gone through the heavens, Jesus the Son of God, let us hold firmly to the faith we profess. For we do not have a high priest who is unable to sympathize with our weaknesses, but we have one who has been tempted in every way, just as we are—yet was without sin. Let us then approach the throne of grace with confidence, so that we may receive mercy and find grace to help us in our time of need. (Heb. 4:14–16)

The efficacy of the intercession of Jesus may be illustrated by the startling transformation Peter experienced. Consider the radical change in his disposition from his threefold denial to his courageous leadership after the ascension. Our astonishment is dissipated somewhat, however, when we recall the warning and promise of Jesus to Peter:

> "Simon, Simon, Satan has asked to sift you as wheat. But I have prayed for you, Simon, that your faith may not fail. And when you have turned back, strengthen your brothers." (Luke 22:31–32)

Jesus offered prayers of intercession for Peter so confidently that their answer was a given. Such efficacy extends through Scripture to all who are Christians as a result of the testimony and ministry of the first disciples. We *know* what Jesus prayed on our behalf in John 17. We *know* God heard, and Christ is even now carrying forward the answers to those petitions. Every Christian should study

Jesus' high priestly prayer and draw utmost confidence from what Jesus prays for himself, his disciples, and us. Read it in personal terms, giving your imagination free rein. Imagine Christ praying that prayer for you. That is *exactly* what he was doing.

For himself and his kingdom work, Jesus prayed:

- that God would glorify him in the crucifixion and beyond, to the full restoration of his eternal glory.
- that he might have full authority to give eternal life to those God granted.
- that eternal life might be empowered by knowledge of the Father and Son.

For his disciples, Jesus prayed:

- that the words given to them might bear fruit.
- that they might be protected and given a unity like that he and the Father shared.
- that they might experience joy like the joy he knew in relation to the Father.
- that they might be sanctified or made holy in the truth of God's revealed Word.

For the disciples' spiritual descendants, Jesus prayed:

- that the apostolic blessing of triune unity might extend to us.
- that we might be so indwelled that the presence of Christ in us is unmistakable.
- that we might go to be with Christ and share his glory.
- that God's love might be in us, just as Christ's presence might be in us.

Such are the prayers of Christ made available in the ascension. These are not speculative affirmations. Each of these petitions, and the theology of sanctification in the church that underlies each, holds unspeakable practical value for every believer.

THE BASIS FOR DIVINE EMPOWERMENT

Though the church may rejoice in the ascension of Christ, insofar as it involves the exaltation of the Messiah to the level of cosmic King and great High Priest, these aspects do not exhaust the riches of that event. Jesus made it clear that his departure was necessary so that the Comforter could come. The Paraclete or the Comforter is the Holy Spirit, who descended on the church on the Day of Pentecost.

Pentecost marks another crucial redemptive historical event in Christianity. It is a new moment in history, but intimately related to the salvation history before and after it. At Pentecost, the Spirit came on the people of God in a new way. The Holy Spirit did exist and was operative before Pentecost. The Old Testament testifies to the Holy Spirit's work in individuals. But at Pentecost a new epoch was inaugurated, in which the entire New Covenant community is endowed by Christ and empowered to fulfill their missionary task.

The Holy Spirit is made known as early in Israel's history as the creation account. When the earth was "formless and empty, darkness was over the surface of the deep" (Gen. 1:2a), it was the Spirit of God that was "hovering over the waters." Repeatedly throughout the Old Testament we hear of the creative power of the Spirit.

The Spirit empowered Old Testament leaders for limited tasks. Judges were strengthened; kings anointed; temple craftsmen gifted; prophets emboldened. Yet the anointing of the Spirit seems to be limited to few individuals, who are gifted for peculiar ministries of leadership.

Two Old Testament texts particularly relate to dynamics of the work of the Holy Spirit in the Old Testament as opposed to the New Testament

Numbers 11 records the endowment of the Spirit on the seventy elders under the authority of Moses. The people who had left Egypt complained about their circumstances to Moses, the mediator of the Old Covenant. This dissension precipitated a crisis for Moses, as he groaned beneath his burden of leadership. In response to the agony of Moses, God commanded that Moses appoint seventy elders to help him. When the elders were properly assembled, we are told:

> Then the LORD came down in the cloud and spoke with him, and he took of the Spirit that was on him and put the Spirit on the seventy elders. When the Spirit rested on them, they prophesied, but they did not do so again. (v. 25)

In response to this distribution of the Spirit to men other than Moses, some of the people (not aware of God's instructions) reacted with discontent. Some viewed this as an intrusion on Moses' sphere of authority. Joshua was particularly vocal in his protest, calling on Moses to forbid the elders from prophesying. In response, Moses asked Joshua, "Are you jealous for my sake? I wish that all the LORD's people were prophets and that the LORD would put his Spirit on them!" (v. 29). Moses' explicit wish is that God would not only enlarge the company of those endowed with the Spirit, but that that company would include the sum total of all the people of God, that the empowering of the Spirit would not be limited to isolated individuals.

This prayer of Moses became the substance of another prophecy, as the prophet Joel declares:

> And afterward, I will pour out my Spirit on all people. Your sons and daughters will prophesy, your old men will dream dreams, your young men

will see visions. Even on my servants, both men and women, I will pour out my Spirit in those days. (Joel 2:28–29)

At Pentecost, the wish of Moses and the prophecy of Joel were fulfilled. Now the Spirit is given to the whole community, down to the maidservants and the menservants. The whole body of Christ is empowered by God to fulfill the Great Commission. Power for mission is granted at Pentecost. The same Spirit that empowered Jesus for his ministry is sent to his people. This was impossible before the ascension. In the ascension, Jesus gains the authority to establish his church in the power of the Holy Spirit.

The final statement Jesus utters before the ascension has to do with the mission of the church and the power of the Holy Spirit: "But you will receive power when the Holy Spirit comes on you; and you will be my witnesses in Jerusalem, and in all Judea and Samaria, and to the ends of the earth" (Acts 1:8).

The seat at the right hand of God is no longer vacant. The coronation of the King of the kingdom of God is no longer a vague hope for the future. The ascension happened. The King reigns—now.

RELATED RESOURCES FROM LIGONIER MINISTRIES

John Gerstner. "Handout Theology: Assurance of Salvation," video or audio series.

Thomas A. Hand. *Augustine on Prayer.*

R. C. Sproul. *Doubt and Assurance.*

———. "Great Men and Women of the Bible," video or audio series, and outline.

———. "Hard Sayings of the Prophets," audio series.

———. "Hebrews Interact," audio series and study notebook.

———. "Keeping in Step with the Spirit," audio series.

———. "Person and Work of the Holy Spirit," audio series.

———. "Salvation Guaranteed," video.

———. *The Invisible Hand.*

———. "The Book of Hebrews," audio series.

———. "The Holy Spirit," video or audio series, and leader guide, or book.

———. "The Lord's Prayer," audio series.

———. "Themes from Hebrews," video or audio series.

Thomas Watson. *A Plea for the Godly.*

I believe . . .
he ascended into heaven . . .
from whence he shall come
to judge the living and the dead.

A Theology of the Future

t the approach of a new millennium in A.D. 999, thousands of people were so fearful of what they perceived to be the end of time that they committed suicide. At the stroke of midnight on December 31, 1999, barring intervention by programmers, many of the world's computers will reset to "zero." And that is not all!

Millennialistic and New Age cultists alike set deadlines for the coming of Antichrist, the return of Christ, and the slide of California into the Pacific. Date-setting prophets have always been around. Jesus told us to expect them. But in anticipation of the year 2000, they have swarmed out of the millennial woodwork. As this book was in preparation there occurred one shocking example of endtimes befuddlement. Mass suicide tested the faith of the Heaven's Gate members. They thought that, by dying at the right moment, they could hitch a ride on a passing alien spaceship that was following the Hale-Bopp Comet in early 1997.

The Lord does not feel obliged to treat the arbitrary turn of our calendars with particular interest. Nor will anyone receive postcards from Hale-Bopp. But in a perverted way, the individuals who took a lethal dose of drugs and covered themselves in purple to await death give Christians cause for shame. We have been told to watch expectantly. At least they did!

THE REST OF THE STORY

We know one thing about whatever date is circled in God's daily planner: The culmination of history will be neither early nor late. Jesus came in "the fullness of time," according to Galatians 4:4. God will bring all things in heaven and earth under one head "when the times have reached their fulfillment" (Eph. 1:10).

> . . . From Whence He Shall Come to Judge
> the Living and the Dead. . . .

Desiring not to be lumped together with date-setters, Bible-believing Christians have lived as though Ephesians 1:10 has fallen out of their Bibles. The incarnation should, of course, be central; all time is defined in light of Jesus' coming. So much of decisive significance took place that it is easy to think that all God intends has been done. But the New Testament does not record a *fait accompli*. The atmosphere of the apostolic age was electrified with expectancy that God would soon complete what he had begun. The apostles worked, taught, and lived as if time were short. Over 1900 years later we should do no less, for the time assuredly is shorter. But there is a woeful neglect of serious investigation into the future hope of Christianity. It is not an area we should slight. Not only does the Apostles' Creed affirm the return of Christ; it is an article of faith in the classic confessions of all Protestant and Roman Catholic churches. We are commanded to *watch*.

There remains another chapter in redemptive history: a future to the work of Christ. He has ascended; he has departed; but he left the world with an unequivocal promise that he will return. The final petition recorded in the New Testament is the plea, "Amen. Come, Lord Jesus" (Rev. 22:20).

When we direct our attention to the study of "last things," called "eschatology," we move into murky theological waters. It is one thing to interpret, reconstruct, and analyze the past; it is quite another to practice a theology of the future. Also, most biblical information comes cloaked in the particularly obscure literary genre of *apocalyptic* literature. This literature is replete with highly imaginative but enigmatic symbolism. Daniel and Ezekiel are apocalyptic Old Testament books; Revelation is the New Testament apocalypse. These visionary documents were written to stimulate deep spiritual thought, even as they resist easy interpretation. Some exegetes are supremely confident that they have the apocalyptic books all figured out. I'm confident that most of them are many miles off course. Let us then proceed with caution to search out the future of the kingdom.

REALIZED ESCHATOLOGY

One approach to the endtimes is to consider them ended. *Realized eschatology* sees nothing left to fulfill. It is the product of liberal theology and skeptical critical interpretation. Since modern theology cannot allow for inspired Bible prophecy or supernatural intervention, future prophetic texts must be dispatched. Out of the old quest for the historical Jesus came the thesis that the kingdom fully and finally arrived in the person of Jesus. What second coming there was could be found in the coming of the Holy Spirit at Pentecost. Others maintain that the destruction of Jerusalem at the hands of the Romans in A.D. 70 signaled the "end of the age." Any present or future "coming" must be purely spiritual. To be sure, this event had great significance as the end of the Jewish age, but it was not the final end of redemptive history.

Variations on this theme have circulated from the pens of such twentieth-century dialectical theologians as Karl Barth, Emil Brunner, and Paul Althaus, though all three abandoned the thesis, due in part to the massive work of Oscar Cullmann on redemptive history.[1]

"SIGNS" OF THE END

The issue centers around the teaching of Jesus on the Mount of Olives, usually called the Olivet Discourse. Matthew, Mark, and Luke, the three Synoptic Gospels, report Jesus' instructions regarding the coming of the kingdom and the future appearance of the Son of Man. Jesus takes the role of true prophet to predict the future. With uncanny accuracy, he foretold the destruction of the Jewish temple and expulsion of the Jews from Jerusalem in A.D. 70.

He also gave "signs" regarding his own future coming and the end of the age. Much speculation has surrounded these precursors of Jesus' coming. These signs were given in response to the inquiry of the disciples: "Tell us, when will this happen, and what will be the sign of your coming and of the end of the age?" (Matt. 24:3). The query is twofold: When will it happen? How will we know it is near? Jesus lists "signs" that will precede his coming with the solemn warning: "Watch out that no one deceives you" (v. 4). He concludes with a command: "So you also must be ready, because the Son of Man will come at an hour when you do not expect him" (v. 44). Thus, the Olivet prophecy comes with both a warning and a command to be vigilant. It focused on events surrounding the destruction of Jerusalem in A.D. 70.

The signs enumerated include wars, famines, earthquakes, false prophets, apostasy, astronomical wonders, violence, and immorality (as in the days of Noah). The signs point to real events and catastrophic upheavals that did occur in the first century.

Concerning the Jews in the Olivet Discourse, Jesus says:

> There will be great distress in the land and wrath against this people. They will fall by the sword and will be taken as prisoners to all the nations. Jerusalem will be trampled on by the Gentiles until the times of the Gentiles are fulfilled. (Luke 21:23b–24)

This passage is usually understood to refer to the destruction of Jerusalem and the expulsion of the Jews under the Roman general Titus. The temple was destroyed and thousands of Jews were killed or taken captive by the Romans. The city was taken over completely in A.D. 135 under Hadrian, after the Romans crushed the revolt of Bar Cochba. This time imperial Roman law made it a capital offense for a Jew to set foot in Jerusalem.

From A.D. 70 to 1948, the Jews were in exile. Dispersed throughout the world, they never lost their ethnic identity. This, in itself, is an anthropological marvel. Jerusalem remained in Gentile hands until 1967. The Arab-Israeli war of 1967 provoked renewed interest in eschatology because of the latter part of Luke 21:24: "Jerusalem will be trampled on by the Gentiles until the times of the Gentiles are fulfilled." Jesus seemed to put a time limit on the captivity of Jerusalem. Biblical scholars in 1967 asked, "Is this war part of the fulfillment of the prophecies of Olivet in that the old city of Jerusalem is now in the hands of the Jews?" Only time will give us a final answer to this question. The debate continues as to whether contemporary Israel as a nation is truly a continuation of biblical Israel.

THE APPEARANCE OF ANTICHRIST

No discussion of eschatology would be complete without reference to Antichrist. Paul warns the Thessalonian Christians not to be premature in expecting Christ's return:

> Don't let anyone deceive you in any way, for that day will not come until the rebellion occurs and the man of lawlessness is revealed, the man doomed to destruction. He will oppose and will exalt himself over every-

thing that is called God or is worshiped, so that he sets himself up in God's temple, proclaiming himself to be God. Don't you remember that when I was with you I used to tell you these things? And now you know what is holding him back, so that he may be revealed at the proper time. For the secret power of lawlessness is already at work; but the one who now holds it back will continue to do so till he is taken out of the way. And then the lawless one will be revealed, whom the Lord Jesus will overthrow with the breath of his mouth and destroy by the splendor of his coming. The coming of the lawless one will be in accordance with the work of Satan displayed in all kinds of counterfeit miracles, signs and wonders. (2 Thess. 2:3–9)

This "lawless one" has been identified by some with the "Beast" of Revelation 13, the Antichrist who will appear prior to the return of Christ. The nature, function, and identity of the Antichrist represents a major theological problem in itself. The question is made more difficult by John's statement that "many antichrists have come" (1 John 2:18). Is Antichrist an individual, or perhaps the culmination of a peculiarly wicked institution? Antichrist has been identified with Nero, Napoleon, Mussolini, Hitler, and a host of other notorious personages. The papacy has been a favorite nominee of Protestants because of the religious and royal character of the office. Luther was quick to give that honor to the pope. The original draft of the *Westminster Confession of Faith* equated the papacy with Antichrist.

Whoever or whatever Antichrist is, it is clear that this role is antithetical to Christ and his kingdom. Paul's "man of lawlessness" suggests that, ultimately, Antichrist is a single human being.

Many other matters of eschatology are constantly debated. Will Jesus come before or after the millennium (the thousand-year reign of Christ on earth)? Will there even be a millennium? What does the Book of Revelation mean by a new heaven and new earth? What and when will the last judgment be? What is the status of people who have died in the interim between the ascension of Christ and his return?

The purpose herein is not to answer questions so much as to suggest that we take more seriously the prophetic dimension of redemptive history. We must be vigilant and diligent in the mission of Christ while our time lasts. The urgency of this day obliges every Christian to the highest call of fidelity to Christ.

RELATED RESOURCES FROM LIGONIER MINISTRIES

John H. Gerstner. "Handout Theology: Eschatology," video or audio series.
———. *Primitive Theology.*
R. C. Sproul. "A Wolf in Sheep's Clothing: Theological Liberalism," video or audio.
———. "Contemporary Theology," audio series.
———. "Hard Sayings of the Apostles," audio series.
———. "The Book of Revelation," audio series.
———. "The Last Days," audio series.

I believe
in the Holy Ghost.

Inward, Onward, and Upward

ach Christian enjoys a double spiritual blessing, observes Andrew Murray. Christ builds a wonderful holy temple for himself in the new, recreated believer. And a still more wonderful holy presence, God's own Holy Spirit, takes up residence. Ezekiel 36:26–27 promises: "I will give you a new heart and put a new spirit in you. I will remove from you your heart of stone and give you a heart of flesh. And I will put my Spirit in you and move you to follow my decrees and be careful to keep my laws." Murray finds himself overwhelmed by Ezekiel's implications and is moved to pray: "Let Thy words 'within you' bow me low in trembling fear before Thy condescension, and may my one desire be to have my spirit indeed the worthy dwelling of Thy Spirit."[1]

The quiet majesty of the divine presence that Murray finds within seems far removed from the Toronto movement, in which the Holy Spirit is manifested in "holy laughter." In charismatic and Pentecostal circles—where worshipers are moved to shouts and tongues-speaking or sudden prostration as they are slain in the Spirit—Murray's Holy Spirit is regarded as suspiciously silent and impotent. God seems hardly in residence at all. Those who feel called by the Spirit to their knees rather than to speaking in unknown tongues wonder, as Martin Luther did of a fellow reformer, if some folks haven't swallowed the Spirit, feathers and all. Orthodox Christians, Pentecostal and noncharismatic alike, should agree on some points regarding the Holy Spirit. The main thing is that the Spirit *is* God, as fully God as the Father and the Son. The Apostles' Creed echoes the *trinitarian* character of the Christian faith.

> I believe in the Holy Spirit. . . .

That the Holy Spirit is regarded as a full member of the Trinity is often passed over. In major theological seminary or university libraries, there are thousands of volumes of theology dealing with the nature and work of God the Father. Perhaps tens of thousands of books deal with Christology. Yet the number of volumes on *pneumatology,* the study of the person and work of the Holy Spirit, is limited indeed. And few indeed are the major studies of trinitarian religion. There is a woeful paucity of serious material dealing with God the Holy Spirit. Perhaps one reason is the subordinate role of the Holy Spirit in redemption. Scripture describes the Spirit as being "sent" by Father and Son. Another problem is the difficulty in constructing concrete categories of definition for the Holy Spirit. The Spirit "blows wherever it pleases" (John 3:8). One can find patterns of activity in the work of the Spirit, but an intangible quality makes the Spirit's personhood difficult to conceptualize. Abraham Kuyper wrote:

> But the Holy Spirit is entirely different. Of him nothing appears in visible form; He never steps out from the intangible void. Hovering, undefined, incomprehensible. He remains a mystery. He is as the wind! We hear its sound, but cannot tell whence it cometh and whither it goeth. . . . There are, indeed, symbolic signs and appearances: a dove, tongues of fire, the sound of a mighty rushing wind, a breathing from the lips of Jesus, a laying on of hands, a speaking with foreign tongues. But of all this nothing remains; nothing lingers behind, not even the trace of a footprint.[2]

Thus, our study of the Holy Spirit must proceed on somewhat precarious footing, but it is well worth the venture. Our effectiveness as Christians, our strength as a church, are inseparably related to our intimacy with the Spirit of God.

THE HOLY SPIRIT IN THE OLD TESTAMENT

The Old Testament word for the "spirit" of God is *ruach*. Like the corresponding Greek term, *pneuma*, it has many nuances, including "wind," "breath," and "spirit." In creation, the *ruach* or "breath" of God is the vital principle of the world (Gen. 1:2). God's breath communicates life to both human and animal kingdoms. The Spirit of God operates in the Old Testament as the basic life principle of the universe. Without the Spirit, there is no life.[3]

In addition to the life that flows from the Spirit of God, the Spirit communicates power to individuals and nations as God directs Israel to her covenant destiny. The effects of the Spirit manifested in the Old Testament are often extraordinary and violent, indicating awesome power. Under the influence of the power of the Spirit of God, men in the Old Testament are known to respond with terror, with trembling, with ecstasy, with fainting, and with exaltation. The Spirit of God is not casual, but overpowering. The New Testament refers to the Holy Spirit in terms of the power and glory of God (Luke 1:35; Rom. 15:13, 19; 1 Cor. 12:4–7; 1 Peter 3:18; see also Zech. 4:6).

In discussing the powerful effects of the Holy Spirit, Jonathan Edwards wrote that the Spirit gives a sense of God's majesty and greatness, "as of a flame infinitely pure and bright, so as sometimes to overwhelm soul and body." Further, the Spirit imparts "a sense of the piercing all-seeing eye of God, so as sometimes to take away the bodily strength; and an extraordinary view of the infinite terribleness of the wrath of God, which has been strongly impressed on the mind, together with a sense of the ineffable misery of sinners that are exposed to this wrath."[4]

The Spirit endows leaders for specific tasks, and operates frequently through the charismatic leadership of Israel. Special powers, talents, and gifts are given to individuals such as prophets, judges, and artisans. The distribution of endowments for ministry reaches its zenith in the anointing of the church at Pentecost.

THE REGENERATING, SANCTIFYING SPIRIT

The power of the Spirit is seen most significantly in the redemptive work of recreation. The Holy Spirit enters the lives of the spiritually dead with a transforming power that brings new life. This is the work of regeneration. *Regeneration* comes from a Greek word meaning "to bear," "to beget," or "to happen" a second time.

Jesus best explained what this means in John 3 when talking with a seeker after God named Nicodemus. Though a Jewish religious leader, Nicodemus was unprepared for Jesus' words, "No one can see the kingdom of God unless he is born again" (v. 3). Jesus announced to this Jewish religious authority the point of understanding they shared—the necessity of entering the kingdom of God. He also showed Nicodemus where his teaching departed from the traditional answer to the question, "How does one enter the kingdom of God?" It is not necessary to keep rituals but one has to become totally new. Without regeneration, no one is capable of "seeing" the kingdom.

Nicodemus raised the obvious question: "How does someone start over like that?" Jesus made this rebirth sound as radical an experience as if one would enter the womb a second time. Jesus elaborated: "I tell you the truth, no one can enter the kingdom of God unless he is born of water and the Spirit. Flesh gives birth to flesh, but the

Spirit gives birth to spirit" (vv. 5–6). Jesus sets forth the necessary condition for new birth into his kingdom. It is a radical experience. One must be born of water and of the Spirit. The allusion to water is open to various interpretations. Likely Jesus just means the first, physical birth from the womb. But his point is the second birth, a birth in which the baby is immersed not in amniotic fluids but the Spirit. Jesus offers some clarification by adding that what is born of flesh is flesh and what is born of Spirit is spirit. Jesus rebukes Nicodemus for his astonishment: "You are Israel's teacher," said Jesus, "and do you not understand these things?" (v. 10). Contained in this rebuke is the clear implication that the concept Jesus is articulating is not a novel idea in redemptive history. This premise is foundational to the biblical concept of conversion. No one is born physically into the kingdom of God. Rather, entrance to the kingdom is dependent on the Holy Spirit. The work cannot be accomplished by birth into a Christian home, baptism, confirmation class, or walking down the aisle. It can only be done by the initiative of God.

In this, *regeneration* is very like resurrection from the dead. In fact, the concepts are used interchangeably in Scripture. Paul does so in his letter to the Ephesians:

> As for you, you were dead in your transgressions and sins, in which you used to live when you followed the ways of this world and of the ruler of the kingdom of the air, the spirit who is now at work in those who are disobedient. All of us also lived among them at one time, gratifying the cravings of our sinful nature and following its desires and thoughts. Like the rest, we were by nature objects of wrath. But because of his great love for us, God, who is rich in mercy, made us alive with Christ even when we were dead in transgressions—it is by grace you have been saved. And God raised us up with Christ and seated us with him in the heavenly realms in Christ Jesus. (2:1–6)

Here is radical change from what a person is by natural birth.

The New Testament sharply contrasts "new" persons and "old" persons. The spiritual state of the old, natural, firstborn person is ghastly. This person is "dead" in sins, is in bondage to sin, and stands under God's condemnation—a child of wrath. In regeneration, the very core of human existence changes. A person not only gains a new disposition or a new perspective; the very quality of personhood itself is new. The secondborn person still sins, but is no longer a slave to sin. The Holy Spirit, in intimate, indwelling communion, liberates. The person is made alive to the things of God. That which once was repugnant now fills with delight. There is a new sense of values, a new lifestyle, a new understanding of self. New life is wrought by the creative energy of the Spirit. The change is so dramatic that Jesus describes it using the metaphor of birth. Regeneration is effected by the same Spirit that "quickened" Jesus in his resurrection. The power of resurrection is brought to bear on a person's life, and the grave of spiritual death opens.

The power of regeneration or "quickening" does not lie within our abilities, self-discipline, or will power. Neither self-creation nor self-recreation is within our reach. Creation or recreation are effected by the "call" of God, who says, "Let there be light" or "Lazarus, come forth." Without God's quickening, no one even desires to be regenerated. Regeneration is accomplished by the power of the Holy Spirit alone.

CONVERSION IN CHRIST

The phrase *in Christ* is one of the most frequently used in the New Testament. When the New Testament exhorts us to faith, we are told to believe *in* Christ; after we believe, we are said to be *in* Christ. However, two different Greek words are used, both translatable by the English word *in*. The word *eis* is used with the sense of moving "into" something when the New Testament speaks of believing in Christ or being baptized in his name (Matt. 28:19;

Acts 8:16). Where the New Testament uses *en* for being "in Christ" (Rom. 8:1), the word means to be *inside* something. There is an identity or union between the believer and Christ. This connection is more intimate than a declared union in which God proclaims us identified with Christ, though a kind of declarative union does operate in the cross. Our union with Christ is real and vital and only possible because the Holy Spirit indwells us. Regeneration not only changes our nature, but also effects a radical change in our relationship to Christ. Prior to conversion, we are "outside" Christ. Faith brings us into and inside Christ. In conversion we can really participate not only in the work of Christ, but in his person as well. We are in him and he is in us as the Holy Spirit not only comes on us, but also dwells in us.

The Either/Or of Regeneration

There is no such thing as a partially regenerate person. Regeneration is not a gradual process, but a spontaneous, creative act of God. There may be a process of preparation preceding quickening and a process of development following it, but the act itself is spontaneous. A person is either "alive" in Christ or not. A heart is either dead to the things of God or not. There may be degrees of Christian growth, but there is a sharp line between the death and life of the Spirit.

However sharp the line may be, it is not always clear to us who has crossed the line. In the first place, there is a difference between *conversion* (using the term narrowly to refer to regeneration) and the *conversion experience.* That is, many know the day and the hour when they become Christians and are often suspicious of people who cannot pinpoint their experience precisely. The latter is frequently true of people who are born and raised in a solid Christian home and church. However, regeneration and the awareness of regeneration are not the same. Regeneration is an objective act of God. Awareness of it is the subjective response of the one regenerated. To be sure, regeneration is a decisive event, but Scripture nowhere enjoins that a person must be immediately aware of the Holy Spirit. Great harm has been done by individuals who wanted to make their own experiences normative for the entire Christian community. The issue from the divine perspective is not *when* a person was converted, but rather *that* a person is converted.

Second, just as two people don't have the same experience, so they may not begin the Christian life at the same spiritual level of understanding. There is also a general grace of God in the lives of unbelievers. Some unbelievers can "outnice" any follower of Christ. Two pagans live side by side. The first has no interest in God, but learns that certain evil practices are destructive personally and consequently avoids them. By all outward appearances, this man is fine and upright, a paragon of virtue. The other pagan has given himself to every form of evil and is enslaved by them all. He has an insatiable lust for illicit sexual relationships; he is an alcoholic, a heroin addict, a compulsive liar, and a thief. Besides all this, he is hooked on cigarettes. The second man is suddenly and dramatically converted to Christ. The immediate influence of the Holy Spirit is evident in his liberation from illicit sex, heroin, lying, stealing, and drinking. His life is radically changed, and the change is apparent to all who know him. But the man still undergoes struggles, perhaps with tobacco. One day Larry Legalist walks up to him and says, "I see you are not a Christian because you smoke." In Larry's eyes, the first man, who is still a pagan, is more conformed to Christ than the second. That is a tragedy, not only because no two Christians begin their Christian life at the same point, but also because no two Christians continue at the same level of sanctification. Regeneration does not automatically convey sinlessness. It gives new life and direction, but it is a new birth that is only the beginning of sanctification. Christians must guard against making their particular level of sanctification the touchstone of everyone else's faith.

New Life in Christ

Regeneration brings new life. When Jesus defined his purpose in coming into the world, he said, "I have come that they [the sheep] may have life, and have it to the full" (John 10:10). There is again some confusion between the New Testament Greek and English. To us, the above statement sounds enigmatic. If Jesus came to bring life, why didn't he limit his mission to visiting the cemeteries of the world? Obviously Jesus has something more in mind than biological vitality. However, two New Testament words can be translated by the English *life*. The term *bios*, from which the word *biology* is derived, generally refers to the normal life processes of breathing, sleeping, or digesting food. The term *zoa*, from which the English word *zoology* is derived, refers to a quality of life as applied by Jesus. Jesus speaks of a new dimension of existence that is qualitatively changed. The source of this life is found in Christ, and he understood his mission in terms of making this new quality of existence available to us. This life is given by Christ through the power of the Holy Spirit. Without the Holy Spirit, people lack this dimension of life offered by Christ.

SANCTIFICATION

The work of the Holy Spirit does not end with regeneration. He does not quicken a person and leave the rest of the Christian life to the person's abilities to learn and morally reform. Regeneration is only the beginning. The goal is conformity to the image of Christ. The Christian is called to mature in obedience and righteousness. This maturing process is also accomplished by the power of the Holy Spirit. The power to grow into holiness, which is what *sanctification* means, is initiated, sustained, and completed by the Holy

Spirit. The Holy Spirit enters the life of a believer to aid him or her in becoming holy.

In justification, a person is counted righteous by God in view of his or her union with Christ through faith. The merit of Christ is imputed or appropriated to the believer. We enter into a relationship with God not on the basis of our own righteousness, but on the basis of *Christ's* righteousness. But justification is not the end of the Christian life. Through the process of sanctification, we are not just counted righteous but are in fact slowly becoming righteous. This process will not be completed in this life, but it certainly begins here, immediately and necessarily at the moment of regeneration.

After the Holy Spirit enters a person's life, there is a sense in which, theologically speaking, the Christian becomes schizophrenic. A tremendous conflict between wills ensues. This struggle is described in biblical terms as warfare between two factions. There is conflict between the natural inclination to sin that characterizes the old man and the desire to please God that characterizes the new man. There is a sense in which life is never so complicated as when a person becomes a Christian. Well-meaning witnesses have dramatically proclaimed, "Come to Jesus, and all your troubles will be over." That sounds appealing, but it is nonsense. When a person becomes a Christian he or she knows both joy and peace unspeakable and also the agony of being thrust into a struggle of almost cosmic proportions. Life takes on new seriousness. Suddenly the stakes are higher. The goal of perfection is set before the Christian. We begin the struggle with the victory guaranteed, but the campaign is filled with failures and defeats. Like the apostle Paul, we do the very things we do not desire to do. The quest for obedience is often a costly one, but worth the price. That is why the Christian can never view God's abiding grace and forgiveness as a license to sin.

In the quest for a holy life, two extremes often become obstacles to sanctification: *quietism* and *activism.* Extreme quietism sees the work of sanctification as totally the work of the Holy Spirit. A person offers no effort or exertion, but quietly waits for the Holy Spirit to change things. This reflects a woeful lack of understanding of the Christian's responsibility to cooperate with the Holy Spirit in sanctification. It also neglects the many admonitions of Christ and the apostles to exercise diligence and self-discipline in seeking holiness.

Activism is the polar opposite of quietism. In this syndrome, a person frantically seeks self-sanctification, constantly endeavoring to live a perfect life through work, without any dependence on the Spirit. This particular method of sanctification is doomed to failure.

The Christian must be actively quiet, or quietly active, in seeking all that is available from the Holy Spirit and in giving all to the goal of sanctification. No final experience in this life ends the struggle. A person can speak in tongues ten thousand times, and still not be free from the influence of sin. A person may hear heavenly voices, see ecstatic visions, and have heartwarming experiences at a thousand altars, but the quest for holiness goes on. There are no easy solutions and no substitutes that can allow a person the luxury of eliminating the daily disciplines of prayer, study of Scripture, worship, fellowship, and service.

None of us have gone beyond scratching the surface of holiness and knowing the ineffable sweetness of communicating with God the Holy Spirit.

"No eye has seen, no ear has heard, no mind has conceived what God has prepared for those who love him"—but God has revealed it to us by his Spirit. The Spirit searches all things, even the deep things of God. (1 Cor. 2:9–10)

RELATED RESOURCES
FROM LIGONIER MINISTRIES

John H. Gerstner. "Handout Theology: Sanctification," video or audio series.

R. C. Sproul. "Building a Christian Conscience," video or audio series, and outline.

"Developing Christian Character," video or audio series, and study guide.

Faith Alone: The Evangelical Doctrine of Justification.

———. "Justification by Faith Alone," audio series.

———. "Keeping in Step with the Spirit," audio series.

———. "Pleasing God," video or audio series, and study guide, or book.

———. *The Holy Spirit.*

———. "The Person and Work of the Holy Spirit," audio series.

R. C. Sproul and others. "Basic Theology," audio series.

The Puritans on Conversion.

I believe in . . .
the holy catholic church;
the communion of saints.

Mighty Army
or Milling Rabble?

I t was a lively discussion group, made up mostly of new Christians. The subject was the institutional church's worship, sacraments, prayer, fellowship, and organization. The church is, most agreed, a corrupt and worthless waste of time. Churches may have had their place, one young man agreed, but now we have God's Word. We certainly don't need a preacher and some old confessions telling us what it means. The Holy Spirit does that. Churches are full of hypocrites, most of whom probably aren't even saved.

No one noticed as Jerry slipped out of his chair. Jerry was a little slow anyway, and he didn't contribute much of importance. Suddenly, a voice drifted to the circle from the darkness of the next room: "I'm sure glad it's just you and me, Lord. But, Lord, you and me together is nice, but it's still kinda' lonesome."

Chapter 11 told part of the story of the work of the Holy Spirit in sanctification. There's more, because the Holy Spirit works inside us most effectively for our sanctification when we are working alongside others. The Lord didn't intend for Jerry to sit by himself in a dark room. He did intend that Jerry bring his quiet insights and simple love into the church. God intends for a miracle to happen each time two or more Spirit-indwelled people come together. They are never really strangers, but family. They are tied to one another and to God—a unity. Alone with God is great. Lonely with God is dangerous to our spiritual well-being.

> . . . The holy catholic church;
> the communion of saints. . . .

The nature of the gospel, said the Scottish divine James Bannerman, makes Christianity a social rather than solitary religion. The Spirit reconciles sinners to God, breaking down barriers of separation erected by the fall. The sinner who was far off is brought near. "The very same work of grace removes the obstacles that hindered his union with other men; and in the fellowship of one faith and one Lord he discovers a new and mightier bond of attachment and union to his fellow believers." Even if the church was not mandated by Scripture, Bannerman added, the dynamics of salvation would make it an inevitable necessity.[1]

A Mightier Bond?

Today there is vast disenchantment with organized religion and the institutional church, particularly throughout Australia, North and South America, the United Kingdom, and Western Europe. One reason is that institutional churches tend to become jarred from their foundations, the revelation of God and the unity that comes only in the Holy Spirit (Eph. 4:3–6). After relativizing their message and politicizing their ministry, many churches are simply helpless infants, being "tossed back and forth by the waves, and blown here and there by every wind of teaching and by the cunning and craftiness of men in their deceitful scheming" (Eph. 4:14). That is precisely what Paul tells the Ephesians is not to happen when they become part of the family of God and bride of Christ: "Instead, speaking the truth in love, we will in all things grow up into him who is the Head, that is, Christ. From him the whole body, joined and held together by every supporting ligament, grows and builds itself up in love, as each part does its work" (4:15–16).

We need to frame any discussion of ecclesiastical problems, then, in the understanding that the visible church is, most profoundly, a social and spiritual institution. The organizational aspects advance the church only so long as they advance the goals Paul outlined in Ephesians 4. The ideal is summarized in the confession: The church is holy and catholic. The positive implication of this is that the church, despite weakness and fragmentation, is still a holy and universal spiritual reality. The negative implication is that when an organization moves away from obedient discipling, faithful teaching, and spiritual worship, it ceases to be the church.

A true, visible church, local or universal, is part of the body of Christ, joined to other churches by belief in Jesus Christ, the eternal Son of God become man, who died in time and space history to pay the debt we owed God for our sin. It is a family of slaves committed to the lordship of the Christ, who physically rose from the dead and reigns in glory. It is a fellowship of worshipers of the one God, who has communicated with us in Scripture. The true church is more than that, but it is at least that.

HELL'S FIRST OBJECTIVE

Even real "churches" have trouble achieving holiness and catholicity. The visible church appears fragmented denominationally and polarized theologically. It has been argued that the church is the most corrupt organization in the world. That is hyperbole. However, to the extent that the charge does hold some truth, we should not be surprised. The church is the most important organization in the world. It is the target of every demonic, hostile attack in the universe. Jesus personally guaranteed that the gates of hell will never *prevail* against the church. He made no guarantee that the gates of hell would not be unleashed against it, however.

Theological liberals lament that the church is saddled with cumbersome, outmoded traditions that ruin the church's relevance as it faces critical issues of society. Conservatives bewail the loss of purity and faith from the New Testament highwater mark. Mainline Protestant denominations have sought pluralism to enable both sides to coexist in some kind of organizational unity. Beyond handshake civility, however, the two groups cannot coexist. Such unity is not "being one" in the sense of John 17, as the Father, Son, and Holy Spirit are one.

No wonder churches are shaken by every sort of issue, from ordaining practicing homosexuals to the place of evangelism and social responsibility. And a church divided by the Jesus Seminar over whether Jesus was a Hellenized intellectual, a peasant revolutionary, or the Son of God cannot possibly enjoy true unity. At stake is whether it is an antiquated society. To avoid the dilemmas, many local churches operate basically on a congregational level, avoiding involvement with sister churches at regional, national, and international levels. That means they sit off by themselves in the dark, cut off from the blessings God intends for the body of Christ.

So, do we write off the contemporary institutional church as an unnecessary vestigial appendage? Do we consider the church an anachronism? Do we add to the proliferation of splinter groups? Do we sublimate doctrine and move in the direction of merger into one monolithic structure that will give organizational union without theological unity? These are hard questions. It is one thing to describe the church. It's quite another to reform it.

NON-NEGOTIABLE PROPOSITIONS

The churches calling themselves "evangelical" have attempted to answer these questions according to the one successful model for cleansing we have—the Reformation of the sixteenth century. The Reformers separated from the Roman Church only after great struggle to reform it from within. There were, however, certain non-negotiable issues. There is no true church, they said, without belief that:

- justification is by grace alone through faith alone (*sola gratia, solus fide*). To reject justification by faith alone through grace alone is to reject the gospel and to fall as a church.
- Scripture is the sole authority in doctrinal matters (*sola Scriptura*). The Bible is the direct revelation of God. Scripture alone binds the conscience of the Christian.

The formal principle that lurked behind Luther's disputation on justification is the same principle that underlies our struggle—the question of authority. Luther's answer emerged at the Diet of Worms on April 18, 1521, in his eloquent articulation of *sola Scriptura*. In Luther's words, "My conscience is captive to the Word of God." Whatever else they thought about Scripture concerning inspiration, interpretation, and canonicity, the Reformers agreed that the ruling authority was apostolic teaching. The Reformation carried with it the cry *"Ad fontes*—to the sources." The New Testament church was the paradigm for reconstruction.

What resulted from their blood, sweat, and tears is visible today. In America alone there are more than two thousand Protestant denominations, all claiming to follow the New Testament paradigm. Obviously, someone is missing something. There is room for differences of opinion in matters of interpretation. On some areas the New Testament is silent or principles must be deduced from its pages for application in modern contexts. But these factors alone cannot be responsible for the theological and ecclesiastical chaos. Rather, we must also include at least two more prominent contributing factors. The first is the deplorable state of biblical illiteracy in the church. Second, and perhaps more important, is widespread de facto rejection of Scripture as the authority in the faith and practice of the church.

The Protestant church rejected the authority of popes and councils. Modern relativistic thinkers reject the authority of the Bible. That leaves only the authority of private opinion. On that highway, the only possible destination is ecclesiastical anarchy.

THE HOLY *EKKLESIA*

When the creed describes the church as *holy* and as a *communion of saints*, it is rooting its categories in the Old and New Covenant community. The covenant community is holy not in the sense that it is intrinsically righteous, but in the sense that it is set apart, consecrated. Israel represents the set-apart community in the Old Testament (Exod. 19:6; Deut. 10:15; Isa. 62:12). In the New Testament this mandate is carried forward into the church (Heb. 12:22–25; 1 Peter 2:5, 9; Rev. 5:10). The word *holy* has roots in the Old Testament concept of division and separation from that which is profane and carries a rich variety of nuances. However, the New Testament church is primarily "holy" in that it is set apart from profanity for a unique relationship with God in Christ, the Holy One of Israel.

The New Testament word for church, *ekklesia*, carries a similar connotation. Literally, the term means "those called out." The *ekklesia* is comprised of those called by God to a peculiar relationship to himself and for a vital kingdom task. Our English word *church* can be traced etymologically to the Greek *kyriache,* which means "those who belong to the Lord," the *kyrios.*

The church is not only "holy" in the sense of being set apart; it is "holy" in the sense of being ethically clean or righteous. Here, the relationship or association with Christ is the basis of holiness, that is, the church is holy insofar as it is in union with Christ and is permeated by the presence and activity of the Holy Spirit. The church is a redeemed community, people called out of the theater of profanity to exist in union with Christ. Hence, the New Testament speaks of the church in corporate and organic terms as the "body" of Christ, or the "people of God," or the "house of God."

VISIBLE AND INVISIBLE

The visible church is an organization or institution. It numbers those whose names appear "visibly" on a church membership roll. Within the visible church, however, there is an *invisible* church. This is not some underground movement. In this church are those whose professions of faith are genuine, those truly "in Christ." The invisible church may include people whose names do not appear on the rolls of visible churches, but exists substantially as a subset of the visible church.

The distinction between visible and invisible churches has historical roots in the remnant of godly individuals who lived within the covenant people of Israel. Jesus also talks about them in the parable of the destructive weeds that were sown with the good wheat (Matt. 13:24–30). Augustine defined the church as a *corpus permixtus,* a "mixed body." The church contains unbelievers, those who worship with their lips while their hearts are far from Christ, and those who worship in spirit and in truth. We cannot discern whose confession of faith ultimately is authentic. Because the true Christian heart is not perceptible to us, but is visible only to God, we speak of the "invisible" church. The fruits of genuine faith need not be obscured, and it is our task to make the invisible church more visible through word and action.

DEFINING THE BODY

The issue of the "true" church is not limited to invisibility. The question of how to define (and find) the true church has prompted much thought. Some have argued that where the bishop is, there is the church. Others argue that where the Spirit is, there is the church. Still others have maintained that where the Word is truly preached and the sacraments are properly administered, there is the church. Since the church has a pilgrim character, some have defined it by its proximity to where God is working in our time. None of these succinct answers seems adequate. One stresses government, another piety, another theology and sacramental perfection, another social relevance. The New Testament church included all these elements. There is no perfect visible church. The New Testament church itself was frequently subject to apostolic rebuke and admonishment. However, we can gain directives from the New Testament as to what a church should be.

A Church Is Ordered

The New Testament churches had visible order and governance. Even the "body" image suggests that the church is more than a spiritual organism that functioned chaotically. The Spirit is the spirit of order. We may disagree about the proper polity, but the propriety of ecclesiastical government cannot be disputed.

That government can lead God's people toward the fulfillment of his kingdom, a disciplined brigade that prepares and purifies its members to meet the challenges of the Christian life. Unfortunately, the church has frequently contributed more to the problem than to the Spirit-led solution. Church history is, in many ways, the story of heresy and extremism. Heresy begets heresy, and extremism is its mother. The corrective to error often becomes a pendulum swing to the opposite extreme.

Self-indulgent worship and a free-to-be-me style of ministry currently in vogue represent such a swing. Particularly in historically strong confessional churches, rigid sometimes autocratic church government has sometimes controlled every aspect of the lives of Christians. Worship was governed by strict conventions. There were plenty of thou-shalt and thou-shalt-not shopping lists. Recent generations have chafed against that style of church. It could have committed the errors of legalism, love of power, hypocrisy, and lovelessness. So we replace one unbiblical model with another. Where the past saw severe discipline and punitive measures, today's churches give virtually no reprimand and exercise virtually no discipline.

Heresy trials in this day? Unthinkable. Instead, creative expressions of faith are applauded for their candor of unbelief. From tightly bound confessional formulas, we have moved to theological subjective pluralism. The cliché remains: "The church that believes everything believes nothing."

A Church Is Fruitful

New Testament concern with piety and visible fruit of the Spirit is also evident. The children of God clearly were called to be transformed people, nonconformists in a profane world. But how nonconformist should nonconformity be? The issue caused major problems in the historical church when it was raised in the monastic movement, the separatist movement, and the modern "relevance" movement. Can we jettison evangelism to express God's love toward the poor and disenfranchised? Should we fulfill covenant obligations in the public or home school? Are we practicing peace when we fight to put a moral issue on the ballot? What level of nonconformity with the secular should we maintain in listening to music or accepting a job that involves working on Sunday?

We are called to relate to the world as righteous people. What that means in individual issues is not always clear, but God has provided a resource center in which to sort out these issues in prayer and study of his Word. That center is a church. To be a Christian is to be a theologian—a student of God and his will. The church is where believers should be nurtured in the practice of correct theology. The contemporary disdain for theological content and emphasis on self-image and emotions were not shared by the apostolic church.

Michael Scott Horton fears that the world has become more profound than the church. While pagans wrestle with the meaning of life, "we're busy organizing ever-greater conferences and conventions so we can talk to ourselves, give each other awards and dazzle each other with the latest evangelical superstars."[2]

GREAT LEADER, MAGNIFICENT PURPOSE

If God was not faithful even when we are faithless and if his Spirit was not stronger than the gates of hell, the future of the visible church would be grim. Perhaps the greatest hope for the future lies in the revolution of the laity. The renewed spiritual depth is being taken back into the local and denominational churches.

To reform the church is difficult, perhaps impossible. But it is a task no Christian can abandon. The church remains the communion of saints in the sense that we are being made holy by the Lord of our church, who will not let us fall. We have a great Leader and a great purpose. Above all else, Bannerman reminds us, the object of the church is "to be the glory of God, in the salvation of sinners, by means of the publication of the gospel."[3]

RELATED RESOURCES
FROM LIGONIER MINISTRIES

John H. Gerstner. "Handout Theology: The Church of Jesus Christ; The Sacraments; Church Government," video or audio series.

———. "Leadership," audio series.

R. C. Sproul. *Commentary on Ephesians.*

———. "Communion of Saints: The Meaning and Mission of the Church," video or audio series.

———. "Evangelism and Missions," audio series.

———. "Ephesians Interact," audio series and study notebook.

———. *Faith Alone.*

———. *Focus on the Bible: Ephesians.*

———. "First Peter," audio series.

———. "Into the Sanctuary: Worshipping God in Spirit and Truth," audio series.

———. "The Bride of Christ," audio series.

———. "The Goal of Christian Living," video or audio.

———. "Themes from Ephesians," video or audio series.

———. "What Are the Sacraments?" audio series.

Thomas Watson. *Plea for the Godly.*

I believe in . . .
the forgiveness of sins;
the resurrection of the body;
and the life everlasting.
Amen.

Victors, Now and Forever

Mrs. Palmer: When my soul is before God, I'm afraid that the other people up there will point their fingers at me and say, "Look at her! How did she get up here? Look how dirty her soul is. She isn't worthy of heaven. There is no good in her. Who does she think she is fooling?"

Counselor: You feel that people in heaven will condemn you?

Mrs. Palmer: Yes, I do. All the good people up there . . . you know, all the saints, will look down on me. They'll know I am dirty, that I don't have a single good thing in me. My mother won't understand either. When she sees what I've done, she'll never be able to forgive me. She may even have nothing to do with me. (Becomes tearful) She was such a good woman that she would never be able to understand me.

Counselor: So you feel that even in death your evilness will separate you from others. You'll be all alone.

Mrs. Palmer: Yes, all alone. All alone.[1]

Forgiveness, resurrection, life. The last three credos in the Apostles' Creed tightly interlock. The affirmation, "I believe in the forgiveness of sins," may be called the quintessence of the Christian faith. At the experiential level this means everything. In the above transcript from a psychologist's counseling session, "Mrs. Palmer" feels an extramarital affair has left her exposed and alone in her guilt before the people she regards as "good." It would make little difference if her Christian counselor were to remind her that those "saints" she fears will condemn her are themselves sinners. She has avoided mentioning the other Person before whom she stands exposed and ashamed—and he *is* good. Beneath her flagellation, Mrs. Palmer recognizes that she is, in fact, existentially guilty. Until she finds peace with the One she has offended, no promises of resurrection and eternal life will seem inviting. Hell is preferable to an eternal heaven of shame.

> . . . the forgiveness of sins;
> the resurrection of the body
> and the life everlasting.

LAW AND GUILT

The word *forgiveness* presupposes real guilt. Forgiveness is meaningless if there is nothing to forgive. To understand forgiveness, we must first understand the meaning of *guilt,* a concept that is open to all kinds of misunderstanding and interpretation. Guilt has a legal connotation in reference to acts or thoughts that transgress a boundary established by law. This law may be an abstract ethical principle or a concrete piece of positivistic legislation. If an ethical norm is violated, guilt is incurred. In the American juridical process, a person is judged guilty or innocent of a particular charge of failing to bring his or her behavior into conformity with the prescribed law. Guilt is inseparably related to law.

Guilt can be incurred in groups, between private individuals, or within oneself. Mrs. Palmer understood that, even if in a neurotic way. The violator of an ordinance or statute is guilty of violating both the principle and the persons behind the principle. Where there is moral law, there is a lawgiver or lawgivers. A criminal charge brought by the prosecutor might be prefaced: "The State of Massachusetts versus John Doe." A person may have violated his or her own person or an "unwritten" law.

Ultimately, guilt involves an individual's relationship to God. After committing murder, David could still write in Psalm 51:4, "Against you, you only, have I sinned and done what is evil in your sight." In God is the ultimate standard and the ultimate tribunal. The relationship involved is the covenant relationship of creature–Creator. Each person is inescapably involved in a relationship with God. A person may despise that relationship or even deny that it exists, but it cannot be wished out of existence. The relationship may be a negative one, a relationship of severe alienation or estrangement, yet it remains a relationship.

The relationship that exists between God and humanity is never neutral. It involves moral obligation and responsibility. Humanity's privileged status in creation carries an enormous burden of moral responsibility to God, to others, to the self, and to the cosmos. Responsibility includes a relationship with the world of nature, in which ecological issues have moral implications. Pollution violates humanity and our environment, but it also violates animals, plants, and other elements of the created order. But most profoundly it violates nature's Designer and Creator. Other relationships somehow involve the sovereign sphere of our relationship to God. We are responsible to God for our behavior toward other people and the cosmos. While the word *theonomy* has fallen into disrepute because some have taken the concept to unbiblical extremes, humanity does exist within the framework of theonomy or "divine law."

THEONOMY VERSUS AUTONOMY

Twentieth-century ethics constantly revolve around questions of personal freedom. Murders have been committed and wars fought in the name of freedom. Freedom is frequently confused with autonomy. *Autonomy* literally means "self-law." An autonomous person is "a law-unto-himself" and is responsible to no one else for personal behavior. Autonomy mandates freedom without restraint. To Friedrich Nietzsche, autonomy meant "master morality." Jean-Paul Sartre idealized existential autonomy. If there is a theistic God, however, freedom without responsibility amounts to immorality. It may be impossible to achieve on a practical level. A society of autonomous people is an anarchy in which the idea of an ethical standard is an absurdity.

Certainly people desire autonomy. However, no human being lives autonomously. Our context is a universe that has been created and is ruled. Jump from a cliff without a hang glider or a parachute and see if you are autonomous over the law of gravity. Only by acknowledging and submitting to laws of physics can a person find the freedom to soar rather than plummet. Whether we acknowledge it or not, we live under a theonomy, under the law of God. The conflict between the desire for self-law and the obligation to submit to the law of God is at the root of the human predicament. The serpent promised Adam and Eve, "You will be like God" (Gen. 3:5). Genesis 3 indicates that the human desire for autonomy and reluctance to bow to the government of God were the central motivations for the fall. All human guilt rests on the foundation of a spirit of disobedience.

This the Scriptures call "sin." Mrs. Palmer found that sin erected barriers all around her. She no longer experienced authentic personhood. Sin's ghastly implications devastated her life. Sin's evil is not merely that rules are violated, but that persons are violated, including the one breaking the law. When I sin against another person, I injure that person, I damage myself, and I bring dishonor to God, whose image we bear. We can describe sin as "finitude," "inauthentic existence," or "psychological neurosis," but such euphemisms cannot mitigate the radical seriousness of the injury effected by sin.

Biblically the term *sin* means literally "to miss the mark." The mark missed is God's standard of righteousness. Theonomy means not only that God operates as Judge, but also that he sets the standard for judgment. It is not within human province to dictate the ethical norm. Rather, that norm is received, and we are responsible to keep it. Something may be pronounced "good" or "bad" ethically as it relates to an ultimate gold standard of perfect acting and thinking. Biblically, that standard is not a matter of human legislation. When we fail to meet the divine standard of righteousness, we experience guilt.

Guilt and Feeling Guilty

It is important to understand the critical difference between guilt and guilt feelings. Guilt refers to something objective, that is, to a status quite independent of feelings. The feeling of guilt refers to something subjective, something that goes on within the emotive makeup of the person involved. The feeling of guilt may, or may not, accurately correspond to situational reality. A person may be guilty of something and not "feel" guilty about it. A person may "feel" guilty, but not actually *be* guilty of any wrongdoing. Lewis B. Smedes observed that Augustine saw himself as "crooked, sordid, bespotted and ulcerous." Hermann Goering sat through the testimony about his crimes and predicted that someday monuments would be erected in his honor. Smedes advises us not to be too quick to try to get over our perceived unworthiness or "shame": "If we feel like flawed persons, it may be because we are in fact flawed. Our shame may be a painful signal that we are failing to be the persons we are meant to be and may therefore be the first hope of healing."[2]

Smedes, of course, knows that not all shame is true, healing, or good. Shame is the fear of rejection, and we have the opportunity to be accepted by the Lord of the universe, One who faced rejection without deserving it or being scarred by it. The answer to shame in either human or divine relationships is grace. "The simplest of all remedies for shame is the discovery that we are in spite of everything accepted by the grace of someone we most need to accept us."[3]

Smedes offers us a delicate balance. If shame feelings are rooted in real guilt, then dealing only with the feeling-level symptoms can cause irreparable damage. The difference between rationalization and forgiveness is that one seeks to deny the guilt while the other seeks to heal it. To confuse the two is the worst kind of Christian Science, a religion that denies that symptoms indicate real sickness, that the pain is unreal. We know better.

Guilt and Conscience

A popular aphorism says, "Let your conscience be your guide." Such philosophy has more to do with "Jiminy Cricket" than with the New Testament. To regard the conscience as the highest tribunal of ethical behavior involves a subtle form of subjectivistic autonomy. The conscience may accuse or excuse us at the feeling level of existence, but it cannot be the ultimate standard of righteousness. After repeated acts of crime, the "professional" criminal can commit heinous deeds without a pang of remorse. Goering reached that point. An oversensitized person has been brainwashed into a false legalism, thinking things are wrong that are not wrong.

The desensitized conscience and the hypersensitive conscience both distort ethical well-being. A seared conscience removes the bars of self-restraint and produces more evil. But so does the act of a legalist who thinks a particular act is evil, when it is ethically neutral, and then commits that act. Such a person has just as surely announced that he or she doesn't care what God thinks. Someone raised in an environment that teaches emphatically that playing bridge is a sin (and I fervently testify that it is not), who believes it is a sin, and who then proceeds to play bridge, is rebelling against God. The guilt is not in the bridge-playing, but in the act of going against conscience, of not caring what God wants.

Scripture does not regard the conscience as the ultimate test of righteousness, but neither does it consider the conscience to be unimportant. The Christian is exhorted to nurture an informed and sanctified conscience (1 Tim. 1:5; Heb. 9:14; 1 Peter 3:16, 21). The carnal mind must be transformed by the Holy Spirit and conformed to the Word of God if it is to become a suitable guide for ethical behavior.

ACCUSED AND CONVICTED

God enters our lives in the person of the Holy Spirit to convict us of our sin. Since God is not the only stimulator of the conscience, we must take special care to discern the difference between true and false conviction of sin. The reality of satanic activity in ethical situations should not be underestimated. Traditionally, satanic activity in the life of the Christian is associated with temptation. Indeed, the Evil One does manifest himself as the tempter. But Satan is also called "the Accuser." One of the most devastating attacks is when our enemy undermines the peace that is ours by right of forgiveness. He dredges up past guilt that God has forgiven and forgotten. He seeks to convince us that personal sins require personal atonement, that the death of Christ on the cross is insufficient. This power of accusation strikes at the very heart of our faith. Nothing is more crucial to our identity in Christ than when our conscience affirms the confession: "I believe in forgiveness of sins."

How can we tell the difference between the conviction of God the Holy Spirit and the accusation of Satan? It is not always easy. "Satan himself masquerades as an angel of light," wrote Paul in 2 Corinthians 11:14. One clue is that the convicting Holy Spirit drives us to God in humility and dependence, but never despair. The Spirit may trouble, upset, or distress us, but his convicting power does not destroy what Christ has redeemed. Satan is brutal; he seeks to paralyze us in servile fear. Against such vicious attacks, Paul cried out: "Who will bring any charge against those whom God has chosen? It is God who justifies" (Rom. 8:33). Paul's confidence rested in the merit of Christ and in God's promise of forgiveness. He could tell Satan to get off his back.

However, given our aptitude for self-deception, the only sure test for discerning the difference between the conviction of the Holy Spirit and that of Satan is the test of Scripture. In the Word of God, we can learn enough about God and about Satan, enough about real guilt and about real forgiveness, to allow us to differentiate truth from lie.

Forgiveness and Feeling Forgiven

Once we have distinguished between real guilt and feelings of guiltiness, a similar distinction needs to be made between real forgiveness and feeling forgiven. Many contemporary Christians have a sensual faith. They ride the tide of rising and falling emotional levels. Christians ought not be devoid of feeling. Ours is a most passionate faith. But the truth of Christ rests on reality, not on our feelings about it.

The issue of reality and feeling is particularly important when we speak about forgiveness. Again, there is an objective–subjective distinction. Real forgiveness from God rests on the declaration God has made. When God declares a person forgiven, that person is forgiven. If a judge decides to show mercy and grant a pardon, removing the penalty for the crime, the defendant is in fact pardoned. He may not feel pardoned; he may still feel guilty (which indeed he is); he may feel he wants to pay for his crime. Yet none of these feelings changes the objective state of affairs—the pardon that has been declared.

The basis of the Christian's assurance of forgiveness is the promise of God. The New Testament tells us unequivocally, "If we confess our sins, he is faithful and just and will forgive us our sins and purify us from all unrighteousness" (1 John 1:9). Repeatedly the Bible assures us that our God is a forgiving God. Assurance of forgiveness should be based on the confidence that God means what he says and does what he says he will do. If God declares that he will forgive our sins if we ask for that forgiveness in the spirit of confession, we can be confident that the sins we have confessed are in fact forgiven.

Feeling may not follow the reality at once. It is difficult to get justification by grace through faith into our bloodstream. We may understand the doctrine intellectually and apprehend something of the meaning of the cross, but still not feel we have received this amazing gift. It is an astonishing thing. The penalty for our sin has already been paid and the judgment that was to be ours has been executed on Christ. This is a staggering thought. Daily we must remind ourselves that there is absolutely nothing we can add to or subtract from the atonement of Christ. If we possess the righteousness of Christ, what more do we need? Our forgiveness rests on his ability, not ours.

We *ought* to feel forgiven, however. There is nothing more blessed than to feel the peace that attends the reality. To experience grace is to know unspeakable joy. Real forgiveness for real guilt stimulates the Christian to songs of praise, thanksgiving, and adoration. We do good works not for penance, but out of gratitude. Jesus indicated this kind of a response when he asked which forgiven debtor will love the benefactor more. The answer was, "The one who had the bigger debt forgiven" (Luke 7:42–43). This ratio of proportionate forgiveness to love may induce the Christian to seek a deeper understanding of the extent to which God has been gracious.

This gratitude is great because we know the difference between a feeling of forgiveness and a feeling of innocence. The peace of forgiveness may feel like the peace of innocence. But forgiveness is not declared innocence; innocence cannot be forgiven. We are treated as innocent, but real forgiveness presupposes real guilt.

Forgiveness and Repentance

Forgiveness is not granted automatically to the world via the cross. God has prerequisites. We must take seriously the biblical call to repentance. That call is not an invitation. God "*commands* all people everywhere to repent" (Acts 17:30b). Repentance is not optional, but obligatory. *Repentance* in the New Testament carries shades of meaning. Literally, the term means a "change of mind." It involves looking at things from a new perspective, viewing sin without rationalization. It includes repudiating sin in a spirit of contrition.

Contrition and Attrition

Historically, there has been considerable debate about *attrition* and *contrition* in repentance and forgiveness.[4] *Attrition* is a "repentance" motivated primarily by fear of punishment. It clings to the mercy of God as a ticket out of hell, an escape from punitive wrath. *Contrition* produces genuine sorrow for having offended God. The New Testament calls us to be contrite in order to receive the forgiveness of God. The spirit of genuine contrition may be best illustrated by Psalm 51. David cries:

> Wash away all my iniquity
>> and cleanse me from my sin.
> For I know my transgressions,
>> and my sin is always before me.
> Against you, you only, have I sinned
>> and done what is evil in your sight,
> so that you are proved right when you speak
>> and justified when you judge. (vv. 2–4)

Here the confession is pointed. There is no attempt by the psalmist to minimize his guilt or to deprive God of the right to judge him. He concludes with the following declaration:

> You do not delight in sacrifice, or I would bring it;
>> you do not take pleasure in burnt offerings.
> The sacrifices of God are a broken spirit;
>> a broken and contrite heart,
>> O God, you will not despise. (vv. 16–17)

Indeed, God does not despise brokenness. His response to contrite penitence is forgiveness.

CHEAP GRACE

Dietrich Bonhoeffer wrote extensively on "cheap grace." Forgiveness is often conceived of in simple terms. Some people believe that God automatically confers grace on everyone, with or without repentance. Such a view of forgiveness sharply distorts the New Testament. It is worse than presumption to demand the forgiveness of God as our due. It makes grace not only cheap, but worthless. "Automatic" grace is grace robbed of its essence, God's voluntary extension of mercy to those who repent. The proclamation that forgiveness is available is at the core of the church's commission. The announcement of forgiveness is good news to those who know the reality of guilt. However, zeal to communicate the goodness of God must never obscure the call of Scripture to earnest and honest repentance.

LIBERATION AND SALVATION

Bonhoeffer struggled with a secularized German church that had left the foundational reliance on God's costly salvation in Christ for an inoffensive, friendly gospel. As a result, German Christians lacked a faith of steel that could withstand the promises and threats of Adolf Hitler's national socialist movement. More recently, the pendulum has tended toward the other extreme. Beginning in the 1960s, various versions of liberation theology made salvation synonymous with political activism in pursuit of justice. This was particularly true in Central and South America, South Africa during its years of struggle over apartheid, and what came to be known as black theology in North America.

Gustavo Gutiérrez defines the purpose of liberation theology in *A Theology of Liberation:* "It is a theological reflection born of the experience of shared efforts to abolish the current unjust situation and to build a different society, freer and more human."[5] Drawing on the theology of European theologian Jürgen Moltmann, Gutiérrez sees theology as a reflection on the historical "praxis," the everyday social political reality of living. As the historical praxis changes, so does theology. Terms such as *salvation, kingdom of God,* and *faith* change with the historical situation. In the Bible and today, their content comes from cultural context, not God. As critical reflection on society changes, theology changes. "In the last analysis the true interpretation of the meaning revealed by theology is achieved only in historical praxis. . . . We have here a political hermeneutics of the Gospel."[6] Theology, then, is a symbolic way of talking about society. Salvation is no longer directly related to sin, faith, and justification, but becomes political liberation.

The frustrating thing about the Roman Catholic liberation theologians, such as Juan Luis Segundo, Gutiérrez, Carmelo Alvez, Emilio Castro, and José Míguez Bonino, is that they have legitimate complaints. Conservative evangelical theology has not adequately dealt with poverty and social justice implications of the church's role in society. Repressive regimes have used the church as a tool for their own ends. But it has been difficult to accept their criticisms and perhaps stand with them in the trenches of ministry when their vision of the gospel is heavily influenced by modernism. They tend to reduce Scripture to a revolutionary saga and salvation to the struggle for socioeconomic liberation.

Gutiérrez begins with the universalistic assumption that all people now participate in Christ and concentrates exclusively on the historical form salvation takes—building a new society. Harvie

Conn notes that "salvation is transformed into economic, political liberation, Christology into love of our neighbor, eschatology into politics, church into humanity, sacraments into human solidarity."[7]

In recent years some of those involved in liberation theology have stepped back and matured in their thinking. In a 1995 study of the religious influences vying for the heart of Latin America, Bonino tries to show himself an orthodox evangelical. Bonino's theology is still slippery, however, and he downplays individual salvation in his quest for a kingdom of concern for the downtrodden. He does not renounce the liberal theology of Moltmann and the Barthian dialectic.[8] The good news is that most liberationist writings of the 1990s have lacked the strident lock-step dialectical Marxism. The failure of the liberationist-backed Sandinistas to institute meaningful justice disillusioned many who had equated Christianity and Marxism. As a whole, however, Bible-honoring Christians should learn to listen with humility and wariness to theologies of liberation. The danger with such movements is that there is a claim to a Christian view of salvation but no actual proclaimed need to be saved from sin through faith in Christ.

RESURRECTION TO LIFE EVERLASTING

We may wax lyrical in praise for the spiritual dimension of humanity, we may exalt our intellectual capacities, we may delight in the uniqueness of the soul; but none of these aspects of human existence negates the stark reality of our physical life.

The phenomenologist has wisely pointed out that the human body is the point of contact or transition between the self and the world. The Marxist has seen that body in terms of economic power. The psychiatrist knows the intimate relationship that exists between body and mind. The physician knows that sickness and pain are realities that affect the status and the well-being of the self. The athlete knows the pleasure in bodily exercise. The married person understands the significance of sexual contact in the human communication of love.

We all live in the context of bodies. But decay and disintegration await the body of every human being. The body is conceived; it is born; it experiences growth and undergoes changes; it ages and moves rapidly toward the experience of death. To call death our "last enemy" (1 Cor. 15:26) is not to use unwarranted hyperbole. That we die is no small thing. The existentialist has said much about what the reality of death means to our existence. Volumes have appeared dealing with the anxiety common to those who contemplate the threat of nonbeing. Our funeral practices betray our inability to face the realities of fear that accompany death.

It is to this dilemma that the Christian faith speaks with clarity and significance. This is no simplistic view that we live on in the "memories" of our loved ones. That is no more consolation than an elaborate funeral or a magnificent tomb. We want life, not monuments. Nowhere does the New Testament appeal to speculative analogies in nature for hope. Because the caterpillar undergoes a metamorphosis on its way to becoming a butterfly is no guarantee that our final destiny will be any better than that of a dead butterfly. Nor is the Christian at the mercy of the spirit medium to gain insight into life after death.

The most astonishing message of the apostles was that Jesus of Nazareth rose from the dead. This resurrection was not seen as an isolated event. The church bases hope for victory over death on the event of the resurrection and the subsequent promise of the resurrected One.

Resurrection and Immortality

Many people confuse the Christian concept of resurrection with the Greek view of immortality (notably, the view articulated by Plato).

The two are not synonymous. Both views affirm that there is continuity of life beyond the grave. But the differences are great. The Greek view of immortality rests its hope for eternal life on its view of the indestructible character of the soul. The soul will continue to live because it always has lived. It existed prior to birth and will continue after the body decays. The soul itself is intrinsically eternal, nonmaterial, and incapable of annihilation. To the Greek, the body is the prison house of the soul. Not until the soul is released from its captor is redemption accomplished.

The biblical doctrine of humanity contains no such pagan concept of immortality. The soul is created. It has no intrinsic self-existence apart from the creative and sustaining power of God. While the Bible teaches that the soul survives death in an intermediate existence, this does not exhaust the Christian hope of eternal life. Where the Greek sees redemption from the body, the New Testament sees redemption including the body. The Christian looks forward not simply to an extended life of the soul, but also to a resurrected bodily existence.

The nature of our resurrected body is a subject of dispute. Apparently the resurrected body will not be identical to the physical, earthly body. However, there will be abiding similarities. We know something about this issue because of what is revealed concerning the resurrected body of Jesus. We know he was seen, that he ate and conversed with his friends. He may or may not have walked through closed doors in the Upper Room, depending on how one interprets Luke 24:36 and John 20:19–20, 26. Jesus gives the invitation to Thomas to touch the wounds in his body, though the record never states whether Thomas did, in fact, touch them (John 20:27–28). Mary did not immediately recognize the risen Christ in the garden (John 20:10–18). Was the confusion due to Mary's emotional distress or because of a substantial change in the appearance of Jesus? The disciples on the road to Emmaus did not recognize Jesus as they walked with him (Luke 24:13–35).

Whatever the resurrected body of Jesus was and is like, it is the paradigm for our own resurrected state. John writes: "Dear friends, now we are children of God, and what we will be has not yet been made known. But we know that when he appears, we shall be like him, for we shall see him as he is" (1 John 3:2). The apostle Paul sheds some light on the question when he instructs the Corinthians regarding the resurrection: "And just as we have borne the likeness of the earthly man, so shall we bear the likeness of the man from heaven" (1 Cor. 15:49). Paul had argued that, even on the earthly plane of existence, there are various kinds of animals, not to mention celestial and terrestrial bodies. He concludes:

> So will it be with the resurrection of the dead. The body that is sown is perishable, it is raised imperishable; it is sown in dishonor, it is raised in glory; it is sown in weakness, it is raised in power; it is sown a natural body, it is raised a spiritual body. If there is a natural body, there is also a spiritual body. (vv. 42–44)

Here, the resurrected body is contrasted with the mortal body in four ways: one is perishable, the other imperishable; one has dishonor, the other glory; one is weak, the other given spiritual power; one is physical while the other is spiritual.

Physical versus spiritual? What in the world (or out of it) is a "spiritual body"? We are accustomed to visualize spirit and body as polar opposites. We think in terms of material and immaterial, extension and nonextension, matter and energy. Obviously, Paul is not thinking like that. In the context of the passage he is speaking of a real body that is in some way analogous to other earthly bodies, yet a body that is qualitatively and ontologically different. We are not told the precise nature of a "spiritual body." Paul describes a future bodily state that is inaccessible to empirical analysis. But the promise remains that God will clothe his people with a new kind of body, one superior to the current model. We will not abide forever as disembodied spirits.

THE SPIRIT–FLESH DICHOTOMY

At many points Paul seems to have been heavily influenced by the Greek dichotomy between spirit and flesh. In such passages as Ephesians 6 he discusses the Christian life as warfare between the spirit and flesh. This is often misunderstood as meaning a negation of the physical life of man.

Part of this misunderstanding can be eliminated if we understand the New Testament usage of the terms *body* and *flesh*. The Greek has two different words, either of which can be rendered by the English word *body*. *Soma* has been incorporated into the English language and is used frequently in the word *psychosomatic*. *Soma* refers to the physical and bodily aspects of man. A psychosomatic illness is one that is caused by psychic disturbance that manifests itself in real somatic or bodily symptoms.

The meaning of *soma* is not difficult to discern. However, the meaning of its companion term, *sarx*, is more troublesome. This term can also be translated by the words *body* or *flesh*, but does not always have specific reference to the bodily dimension of life. Particularly when Paul sets the term *spirit (pneuma)* in opposition to *flesh (sarx)*, he uses the term figuratively. Paul describes a warfare between two qualitatively different lifestyles. The lifestyle of the godly, spiritual person, whose life is informed by the Holy Spirit, is contrasted with the person whose lifestyle is manifested in natural and carnal fleshly goals and behavior. This is not warfare between mind and body or between the spiritual and physical. Carnality or "fleshliness" in this context describes a negative quality of life. Here, the mind and soul, the physical and the spiritual aspects, are described as corrupt.

The Scriptures do not allow an intrinsically negative value to be attached to physical things. God created a physical world and gave it his benediction, calling it "good." The promises of Old and New Covenants include physical blessing. Failure to understand this has caused the church to distort the message of the gospel. Infected by Platonic ideas, the church has often demeaned the value of the physical, and we are left with a negative view of creation, physical needs for enjoyment and sexual fulfillment, and other beautiful and good aspects of the created order. The physical was created by God and will be redeemed by God.

We look not to the destruction of the heaven and earth, but to renovation—a new heaven and earth, where God's creation will be redeemed, not obliterated.

RELATED RESOURCES
FROM LIGONIER MINISTRIES

John H. Gerstner. "Handout Theology: Eschatology," video or audio series.
R. C. Sproul. "Benchmarks: Five Qualities of the Mature Christian Life," audio series.
———. *Essential Truths of the Christian Faith.*
———. "Doctrine of Sin," audio series.
———. "James Interact," audio series and study notebook.
———. "Modern Atheism," audio series.
———. "Surprised by Suffering," video or audio series, or book.
———. "Last Days," audio series and outline.
———. "The Book of Revelation," audio series.
———. "The Drama of Redemption," video or audio series.
———. "The Goal of Christian Living," video or audio.
———. "Themes from James," video or audio series.
Solomon Stoddard. *The Safety of Appearing on the Day of Judgment in the Righteousness of Christ.*
Thomas Watson. *The Mischief of Sin.*

Notes

Chapter 1: Confess or Profess?

1. The apostle Paul describes the newness of life in several passages, among them Rom. 6:4; 2 Cor. 5:14–16; Gal. 6:14–15; Eph. 2:10, 15; Col. 3:9–10. Read Romans 8 to see just how radical Paul believes this new creation to be.

2. "In the synagogue there was a man possessed by a demon, an evil spirit. He cried out at the top of his voice, 'Ha! What do you want with us, Jesus of Nazareth? Have you come to destroy us? I know who you are—the Holy One of God!' 'Be quiet!' Jesus said sternly. 'Come out of him!' Then the demon threw the man down before them all and came out without injuring him" (Luke 4:33–35; compare with Luke 8:28).

3. See Pss. 1:2; 16:3; 35:9; 37:4; 43:4; 111:2; 112:1; 119:16, 24, 35, 47, 70, 77, 92, 143, 174.

Chapter 2: God-talk

1. *Enneads* 6.9.3–4.

2. Herman Melville, *Moby Dick* (New York: Oxford University Press, 1955), p. 161.

3. Martin Luther, *The Bondage of the Will*, trans. (Westwood, N.J.: Revell, 1957), pp. 66–68.

4. Emil Brunner, *The Christian Doctrine of God: Dogmatics: I* (London: Lutterworth, 1958), p. 123.

5. Helmut Gollwitzer, *The Existence of God as Confessed by Faith* (Philadelphia: Westminster, 1965), p. 153.

Chapter 3: Spiritual Genetics

1. For a more detailed discussion of the New Testament meaning of brotherhood, see von Soden, *"Adelphos,"* in Kittel, *Theological Dictionary of the New Testament* (Grand Rapids: Eerdmans, 1985).

2. Geerhardus Vos, *Biblical Theology* (Grand Rapids: Eerdmans, 1948), p. 96.

Chapter 4: Of Chaos and Dignity

1. Edward J. Carnell, *An Introduction to Christian Apologetics* (Grand Rapids: Eerdmans, 1948), p. 22.

2. Herbert W. Richardson, *Toward an American Theology* (New York: Harper & Row, 1967), p. 123.

3. Ibid.

CHAPTER 5: THE MAN WHO IS THE ISSUE

1. The views for which Paul C. McGlasson was so severely censured can be found in his book *Another Gospel: A Confrontation with Liberation Theology* (Grand Rapids: Baker, 1994). A similar book by a former student of Rudolf Bultmann offers insights into the academic research and publication and New Testament scholarship biases. See Eta Linnemann, *Historical Criticism of the Bible* (Grand Rapids: Baker, 1990).

2. See Norval Geldenhuys, *Commentary on the Gospel of Luke,* The New International Commentary on the New Testament (Grand Rapids: Eerdmans, 1951).

3. Oscar Cullmann, *The Christology of the New Testament* (Philadelphia: Westminster, 1959), p. 182.

4. Ibid., pp. 166ff.

5. Karl Barth, *Church Dogmatics,* vol. 4 (Edinburgh: T. & T. Clark, 1956), pp. 230ff.

6. Cullmann, *Christology,* p. 161.

7. Paul M. van Buren, *The Secular Meaning of the Gospel* (New York: Macmillan, 1963), p. 48.

8. Cullmann, *Christology,* p. 199.

9. Ibid., p. 200.

CHAPTER 6: THE VIRGIN HAD A WHAT?

1. Oscar Cullmann, *Salvation in History* (New York: Harper & Row, 1967), and John Warwick Montgomery, *History and Christianity* (Downers Grove, Ill.: InterVarsity, 1964).

CHAPTER 7: SUFFERING SERVANT FOR ME

1. G. C. Berkouwer, *The Work of Christ* (Grand Rapids: Eerdmans, 1952), pp. 166ff.

2. Such covenants included a *preamble* that identified the king, a *historical prologue* summarizing the history of the relationship between the king and the vassal, and the *stipulations.* Stipulations included the detailed obligations, provision for deposit in the temple and periodic public reading, the list of gods as witnesses, a formula of blessings for keeping the covenant and curses for breaking it, the formal oath, and the ratification ceremony.

3. See George E. Mendenhall, *Law and Covenant in Israel and the Ancient Near East* (Pittsburgh, Pa.: Biblical Colloquium, 1955), and Meredith Kline, *By Oath Consigned* (Grand Rapids: Eerdmans, 1968).

4. Hans Küng, *Justification* (New York: Nelson, 1964), p. 149.

5. Berkouwer, *Work of Christ,* p. 182.

CHAPTER 8: GRAVE WITH A VIEW

1. Rudolf Bultmann, *Kerygma and Myth,* ed. Hans Wermer Bartsch (New York: Harper & Row, 1961), pp. 3–5.

2. Research on the Dead Sea Scrolls has given Christians a leap in their understanding and defense of the New Testament. Found in the Qumran community's hidden library are actual first-century New Testament fragments. Using methods of papyrology and paleography, Jose O'Callahan dated and identified fragments from Mark 4, 6, and 12 (A.D. 50), Acts 27 (A.D. 60+), and Romans 5, 1 Timothy 3, 2 Peter 1, and James 1 (all A.D. 70+). Some of these fragments are too small to be positively identified, but at least some are definitely from these texts. They add a powerful argument that these writings originated with the generation that knew Jesus personally.

3. See Clark H. Pinnock's discussion of this issue in *Biblical Revelation* (Chicago: Moody, 1971). See particularly his treatment of "the fideists," pp. 38ff.

4. At the heart of the issue with Bultmann is the question of the Judeo-Christian approach to history. It is not without reason that Bultmann's approach has frequently been labeled as Neo-Platonic or neo-agnostic, in that redemption is often removed from the plane of real history.

5. An interesting comparison could be drawn between Paul's treatment of the resurrection in 1 Corinthians 15 and Immanuel Kant's moral argument for the existence of God. Kant argues from a practical basis what is necessary for meaningful ethics. Paul does this implicitly, but goes beyond Kant to root his faith in history rather than practical necessity.

CHAPTER 9: *THERE FOR US*

1. John magnifies this concept when he distinguishes between the descent of Christ from heaven and his ascent to heaven. See Johannes Schneider's treatment of this under "*Baino*" in Kittel, *Theological Dictionary of the New Testament.*

2. See John Murray, *Principles of Conduct* (Grand Rapids: Eerdmans, 1957).

CHAPTER 10: *A THEOLOGY OF THE FUTURE*

1. See particularly *Christ and Time* (New York: Gordon Press, 1977) and *Salvation in History* (New York: Harper & Row, 1967).

CHAPTER 11: *INWARD, ONWARD, AND UPWARD*

1. Andrew Murray, *The Spirit of Christ*, rev. ed. (Minneapolis: Bethany House, 1983).

2. Abraham Kuyper, *The Work of the Holy Spirit* (Grand Rapids: Eerdmans, 1956), p. 6.

3. Walther Eichrodt, *Theology of the Old Testament*, vol. 2 (London: SCM, 1967), pp. 46ff.

4. Jonathan Edwards, *The Works of President Edwards*, vol. 3 (New York: Carter, 1879), p. 303.

CHAPTER 12: *MIGHTY ARMY OR MILLING RABBLE?*

1. James Bannerman. *The Church of Christ*, vol. 1 (Carlisle, Pa.: The Banner of Truth Trust, 1960), pp. 19ff.

2. Michael Horton, *Putting Amazing Back into Grace* (Grand Rapids: Baker, 1994), p. 24.

3. Bannerman, *The Church of Christ*, 1:59.

CHAPTER 13: *VICTORS, NOW AND FOREVER*

1. Leroy Aden and David G. Benner, eds., *Counseling and the Human Predicament: A Study of Sin, Guilt, and Forgiveness* (Grand Rapids: Baker, 1989), p. 108.

2. Lewis B. Smedes, *Shame and Grace: Healing the Shame We Don't Deserve* (New York: HarperCollins, 1993), p. 31.

3. Ibid., p. 60.

4. This issue is particularly relevant to the Reformation dispute concerning the Roman Catholic sacrament of penance. Full discussion of this matter would require a more extensive theological treatment than is possible here.

5. Gustavo Gutiérrez, *A Theology of Liberation* (Maryknoll, N.Y.: Orbis, 1988), p. xiii.

6. Ibid., pp. 10–11; see also p. 54.

7. Harvie M. Conn, "The Mission of the Church" in Carl Armerding, ed., *Evangelicals and Liberation* (Nutley, N.J.: Presbyterian & Reformed, 1977), p. 82.

8. José Míguez Bonino, *Faces of Latin American Protestantism* (Spanish edition 1995; Engl. trans., Grand Rapids: Eerdmans, 1997). See esp. pp. 108–27.

R. C. Sproul is founder and chairman of Ligonier Ministries, a teaching ministry that produces Christian educational materials designed to fill the gap between Sunday school and seminary. Beginning as a small study center in Ligonier, Pennsylvania, this ministry moved in 1984 to Orlando, Florida. With a staff of more than fifty people, Ligonier provides laypeople and pastors with substantive materials on theology, church history, Bible study, apologetics, and Christian ethics.

In addition to more than forty books and three hundred audio and video teaching series for adult study, R. C. has written two children's books, a novel, and a biography. He has also edited several volumes, including a festschrift for John H. Gerstner, a seminary textbook, and the *New Geneva Study Bible*.

Ligonier's radio program, "Renewing Your Mind," features R. C. and is broadcast nationally five days a week. Ligonier Ministries produces a monthly periodical, *Tabletalk*, has its own web site (see page 4 for the address), and sponsors several seminars a year, the largest of which is held in February in Orlando.

R. C. has taught hundreds of thousands of people through books, radio, audio and video tapes, seminars, sermons, seminary classes, and other forums. His goal is to help awaken as many people as possible to the holiness of God in all its fullness. His vision is that believers would apply truth to every sphere of their lives.

In 1994 *Christianity Today* asked a select list of critics, "What theologian or biblical scholar has most shaped your Christian life?" Third on the list (and the only American in the top four) was R. C. Sproul.

Dr. Sproul, a graduate of Westminster College, Pittsburgh Theological Seminary, and the Free University of Amsterdam, is professor of systematic theology and apologetics at Knox Theological Seminary in Fort Lauderdale and is ordained in the Presbyterian Church in America.